Florence
Nightingale

THE LADY OF THE LAMP

Florence Nightingale

THE LADY OF THE LAMP

Basil Miller

BETHANY HOUSE PUBLISHERS
MINNEAPOLIS, MINNESOTA 55438
A Division of Bethany Fellowship, Inc.

CONTENTS

Chapter 1

STRAWS IN THE WIND

"HE GAVE SOME to be apostles," and others nurses, but the divine call was the same though tasks were diverse. Paul was an apostle to the Gentiles and Florence Nightingale was an apostle of nursing, but God ordained each for his noble task—a task fulfilled under the divine leadership.

Susannah Wesley served God by giving birth to sons who changed their generations. David Livingstone, God's missionary, opened the Dark Continent to the Gospel. Augustine was God's great thinker, and Ann Judson was God's heroine of Burma. Florence Nightingale was also divinely appointed and, attired in a nurse's uniform, performed a task as holy as that accomplished by Martin Luther when he hurled his vindictives at Rome and shouted, *The just shall live by faith!*

These divinely appointed men and women left their mark on the centuries. William Carey was a lonely missionary in India, but his spiritual energy culminated in the modern missionary movement, which has reached all nations with the Gospel story. In childhood Florence Nightingale heard the challenge, *Be a nurse . . . be a nurse,* and eventually she began a movement under whose banner the tender hands of gentle women cool the fevered brows of the sick and whisper words of comfort to the dying. On the battle-field, where Florence Nightingale gained her fame as "the lady with the lamp," the Red Cross nurse is a symbol of mother, sweetheart, sister and spiritual adviser to our wounded sons and loved ones.

How great would have been the world's loss had not Florence Nightingale followed the divine gleam and been obedient to the heavenly vision. We hail Florence Nightingale as the mother of nursing, the lady whose lamp glows on sickbeds and field hospitals. Her spirit is present in ambulances, hospital planes, and warships consecrated to the care of the wounded and sick.

Florence Nightingale achieved a just fame. Gladly did she offer on God's altar all that she was or possessed that this ideal might be scattered throughout the nations. The influence of friends, the demands of parents, and the glittering wealth with which she was early surrounded could not tempt her eyes from the gleaming light which shone upon her path, and with Paul she could say, "I was not disobedient to the heavenly vision."

Seldom does history tell the intimate story of so charming, distinctive and capable a young woman as Florence Night-ingale, reared in luxury and at home in the highest social circles, who turned her back upon all this and performed the lowest and most menial task of her day. Florence was motivated by a pure desire, an exalted passion, to ease the suffering of the afflicted and wounded, that she might hear the master say, "Inasmuch as ye did it unto the least of these, ye did it unto me."

Florence forsook grandeur and elegance that she might help the suffering world. Her soul thrilled with the joy of pleading the cause of the neglected, the poor and hospital-ized. She fought diplomatic and political battles worthy of a general, and her heroic efforts in these fields matched the bravery she demonstrated when nursing the wounded during the war of 1854-55 in the Crimea. Seeing a great need, she attempted to meet it by organizing the Red Cross. She was confident that the Almighty would come to her aid.

Florence's parents were wealthy and high born. At the age of nine her father, William Shore, inherited from his great uncle, Peter Nightingale, extensive properties, including a lead mine, which added substantially to the revenue of the estate. At the time he married he was not only a cultured gentleman but also a rich man, who had studied at Cambridge and Edinburgh. An original (and often dominating) thinker, he was in advance of the estate owners near him.

His generosity supported a school where the boys and girls of the neighborhood could learn to read and write at a cost of only a few pennies weekly. When parents failed to take advantage of his liberality by not sending their children, he chided them with the rod of his wrath. His tongue, moreover, was far from gentle.

He selected as his bride lovely Frances Smith, the daughter of an individualistic father who believed that in matters of conscience and thought one must always be free. Grandfather Smith, as Florence was to learn, tried earnestly to relieve the underprivileged and was touched with pity for the unfortunate. From him, as well as from her father, the future nurse was to inherit an indomitable will, the vision of a social reformer, and an independence that heeded neither the ire of generals nor the dictates of kings.

When Florence's parents spoke their nuptial vows, as became their wealthy status, they went abroad for their honeymoon, which lasted two years. During this time, while they were vacationing at Naples, the eldest girl was born, and forthwith Father Nightingale named her Frances Parthenope, the first name honored her mother and the second was the ancient Greek name of the city in which the child was born.

By May 12, 1820, Florence's parents had meandered to Florence, Italy, where they lived in the beautiful Villa

Comambia. Here the girl opened her eyes to the light. Her father forthwith called his child after the city, and henceforth the world has always known her as Florence.

In later years, Italy, her birthplace, or England, her native land, could not rightly claim her as their own, for the world was to take her to its bosom as a beloved daughter.

When the family returned to England, they settled first at Lea Hall, inherited from the great uncle. But wealthy William found the house not altogether satisfactory and the location, delightful at some seasons of the year, was not suited as a winter home, for the countryside was bleak and desolate. Seeking a more pleasant home and one that could evidence his wealth and please his vanity, William discovered Lea Hurst, not far distant, where he built his home— a home which in the years to come, however, could not hold Florence after she had caught the heavenly vision.

Lea Hurst had the charm of Elizabethan architecture, and the greenery which crept over its stone walls gave it the air of being a quaint old castle. The picturesque chimneys, gables, mullioned windows and latticed panes added to its quaintness.

"High as Lea Hurst is," writes a visiting friend, "one seems on a pinnacle with clouds careening around one. Down below is a garden with stone terraces, the planes of these terraces being perfectly gorgeous with masses of hollyhocks, dahlias, nasturtiums, geraniums, etc. Then a sloping meadow, losing itself in a steep wooded descent (such tints over the woods!) to the River Derwent, the rocks on the other side of which form the first distance, and are of red color streaked with misty purples.

"Beyond this, interlacing hills forming three ranges of distances; the first deep brown with decaying heather, in some purple shadow, and the last, catching pale, watery sunlight."

From this home Florence went to the Crimea, from which she returned with the laurels of victory when the war was over. At Lea Hurst she spent many of her later years, and on a balcony opening from her second-floor room she often addressed the crowds of visitors who came to see her. In the center of the front garden was a small building, known as the "chapel," which Florence's father retained when he built his mansion, for it was one of several old Norman oratories yet remaining in the district.

It was here that Florence in later years held the Sunday afternoon Bible class she organized for the young women of the neighborhood.

The region where she spent her girlhood was historic. In a stately mansion near by once dwelt one of the conspirators who sought to release Mary, Queen of Scots, and through the winding lanes and homes the officers of good Queen Elizabeth had searched for the traitors.

The estate was wooded, and in her childhood, as in later years, Florence loved to travel a long avenue that led over hills and through forests. Today this is proudly described as "Miss Florence's favorite walk." The music of the Derwent waters was heard in the wooded glades, and often in the midst of hardship, Florence remembered the waves in the strait.

"How I like on a stormy night," she would say, "to hear the ceaseless roar. It put me in mind of the dear Derwent. How often I have listened to it from the nursery window."

Delightful though William found Lea Hurst to be, he also, as wealthy men are wont, discovered disadvantages. In the winter the wild winds blew—winds too fierce for the rich man and his children. William asked himself and others, "Where is the country that is habitable for twelve successive months? For my part, I think, that provided I could get about two thousand acres and a house in some neighboring country where sporting and scenery were in tolerable abundance, and the visit to Lea Hurst were annually confined to July, August, September and October, there all would be well."

This Florence later learned was the talk of the idle rich, for satisfaction is found not in environment but in spiritual status, not in climate but in the heart. Looking for such a location, William eventually discovered the ideal haven for his family at Embley in Hampshire, which edged New Forest. The mansion was more stately—his revenues had increased and his house must match his purse—than Lea Hurst, and was surrounded by lovely old oaks, beaches, laurel and rhododendrons.

Being farther south and free of the Derbyshire breezes, flowers bloomed profusely. June at Embley was unforgettably beautiful. Primroses burst in March, and a long road, rhododendron-flanked, winded through the estate. Florence could not forget the flowers which she had loved in childhood, and in later years Florence often drove to London's famous rhododendron park that she might recapture something of the joy.

At the age of six Florence was blessed with two lovely homes, Lea Hurst, in which she spent the summer, and Embley, a refuge during cold weather. Both homes were in the country, and the girl found delight in trees, flowers, birds and the simple farm folk who learned to love the girl, for she took a deep interest in their lives and was always eager to help in time of sickness or need.

Mounted on her pony one day (she often rode through the countryside), Florence and the vicar with whom she was riding came upon a scene which disturbed the serenity of the farm folk. Ordering her pony to stop, she looked at the sheep.

"The sheep are scattered," she exclaimed, "and old Roger can't seem to collect them. Where is Cap, his dog?"

The shepherd, Roger, approached and said sadly, "The boys broke his leg by throwing stones. I'll need to put an end to him."

"Oh, no! no! Where is he?" asked Florence, who loved animals.

Pointing to an old shed down the road, the shepherd said, "But you can't do anything, missy. I'd best put him out of his pain tonight."

Turning to the kindly vicar, Florence said, "We must do something," and spurred her pony to the shed in which the beautiful collie lay. The bewildered vicar followed.

They found the collie lying on the floor, and after examining the leg, the vicar declared, "His leg is not broken. He can be saved by nursing."

The cleric and the child heated water and made compresses from the shepherd's old cast-off shirt. Gently they laid the hot cloths on the dog's injured limb. Later, when the shepherd returned with a rope to hang the dog, the animal nuzzled him with a whine.

"Throw away your cord!" said the little nurse joyously. "Cap will get well!"

Florence had won her first nursing case, for Cap did get well. Years later the vicar, writing to the nurse, then famous, said, "I wonder whether you remember how, twenty-two years ago, you and I averted the intended hanging of poor old shepherd Smither's dog Cap? I can recollect the pleasure which the saving of the life of a poor dog then gave to your young mind. I was delighted to witness it. It was to me not indeed an omen of what you were about to do and be (for of that I never dreamed), but it was an index of that kind and benevolent disposition of that I Corinthians 13 which has been at the root of it."

When a girl, Florence gave evidence of her interest in medicine. After making a tiny book the size of a postage stamp, she recorded in it this prescription: "16 grains for an old woman, 11 for a young woman, and 7 for a child."

She bandaged her "injured" dolls and cared for them with all the faithfulness of a tenderhearted mother. Often when neighborhood animals were hurt or sick, Florence was their nurse and physician. These "straws in the wind" indi-

cated the direction in which the wind of her interests was
blowing.

Meanwhile Florence's father was diligently supervising
her education. She and her sister Parthe were near the same
age, and studied together. The girl's father held advanced
views on the education of women. He plunged beneath
superficialities and sought hidden realities. He would have
none of those theories which would frustrate such a brilliant yet youthful mind as his Florence possessed.

Florence and her sister studied the usual subjects in the
curriculum of an English girl in a wealthy home. Florence's
courses included music, drawing, embroidery and modern
languages. Eventually, however, her father decided that she
should study constitutional history, a subject which the men
of the day considered too deep for female minds. Her
father determined that she study Greek and Latin, and
brilliantly, the young girl read Tasso, Aristo and Alfieri.
She also translated such works as *Phaedo*, the *Crito* and
the *Apology*.

Florence analyzed Stewart's *Philosophy of the Human
Mind* and then absorbed Roman, Italian, German and Turkish history. Her father realized his dream, and his Florence
and older sister were far better trained than the majority
of women who lived during the first part of the nineteenth
century. An excellent student, Florence sought new fields
to explore, one of which was mathematics, concerning which
her sister wrote:

"Florence has now taken to mathematics, and like everything she undertakes, she is deep in it and working very
hard."

A few years later the brilliant young student discussed
geology with a famous authority on the subject, and, apply-
ing her keen insight to the problem of the earth's formation,
she challenged the expert. To her left, at the same dinner
table, sat an Egyptologist with whom she discussed ancient
inscriptions until, when she quoted whose works she had

studied in the original, her erudite dinner partner, too, had to beat a verbal retreat.

"A capital young lady," each authority admitted, "if she hadn't floored me with her Greek and Latin."

Florence did more than revel in the ancient writers and enjoy the fruits of her father's inherited wealth. In fact, aside from her studies, she was more keenly interested in other pursuits than having pleasure with agreeable social companions. Her mother, as was the custom of wives of the wealthy, busied herself with the needs of the poor and sick. Florence accompanied her mother on these trips of mercy, and these experiences aroused the girl's sympathy for the afflicted and destitute. This understanding of the problems of the poor enabled her to enter easily into the problems of the Crimean soldiers.

Florence was quick to see that a pet could cheer a sick child or that a bouquet of flowers could bring hope to an adult. In later years she reflected on her experiences and demonstrated the healing power of a kind act. In fact, many years later in the Crimea she began to recover speedily from a serious illness when someone gave her a bouquet of flowers.

The years passed swiftly, and many unforgettably happy hours were spent in walks, visits to the sick and Greek, Latin, English and modern-language courses in the private school-room lavishly furnished by her father. When Florence was seventeen, these studies were completed, but a well-to-do Englishwoman's studies were not terminated properly until a trip abroad had given her a final polish. Therefore, on September 8, 1837, the Nightingale family crossed from Southampton to Havre for a trip to the Continent.

The days abroad were rich with pleasure and association with distinguished company, as befitted William's prosperity and lavish generosity. The family's social position, to say nothing of their financial rating with Lloyds of London, gave them access to people of culture and families less intellectually distinguished but more prosperous financially than they. Leisurely the Nightingales jaunted through France, visiting such historic places as Chartres, Blois, Tours, Nantes, Avignon, Toulon and the wicked but beautiful French Riviera, where they remained during December, 1837, and January, 1838.

Reluctantly William left the region of the blue Mediterranean because of Florence's keen interest in newer sights, and yielding to her pressure, the family went to Genoa. They then spent a month in Florence, namesake city and birthplace of the family's younger daughter. Urged by the warm weather, they turned northward to Italy's lovely lakes and Switzerland's snow-crowned peaks, and arrived in Paris on October 8, 1838.

In her diary, which Florence kept diligently, she refers to the scenery, social conditions, works of art, land systems, and above all charitable institutions which she observed. Her accounts are detailed, and she reveals her interest in figures and statistics by recording in orderly columns the distance in leagues between cities and the day and hour of arrival and departure.

"A stirring day," her notes say of September 12, 1838, for news had reached Geneva, where they were then staying, that the Emperor of Austria had declared amnesty in Italy. It was indeed a significant day, "the most stirring which we have ever lived." She tells also of the party which they had attended that evening when the Imperial Decree was read. Her brilliant mind could not be satisfied with social trivialities when she was in an atmosphere of ideas.

"All Sismondi's political economy seems to be founded on the overflowing of heart," she wrote of a noted historian whom she had met through a friend's courtesy. "He gives to old beggars on principle, to young from habit. At Pescia he had three hundred beggars at his door one morning. He feeds mice in his room while he is wrestling with historians."

Greedily the girl observed the scenes in her native Florence, but this was not the city to which she dedicated her heart, though she speaks of it as a place she "would not have missed for anything." It was here that she revealed her skill in nursing, for an Englishwoman, who later became a foreign princess, fell ill and Florence had the joy of nursing her to health.

It was Genoa—glorious Genoa—that won her heart. Here she met the nobles in their luxury and idleness, the poor in their poverty. Here she reveled in lavish Italian palaces. She enjoyed court functions and courtly entertainments, beautiful music, and the pleasure of discussing political economy with would-be Italian specialists. The Italian opera fascinated her. She attended all the performances and kept a diary devoted exclusively to the programs.

"I should like to go every night," she confessed in a note. Having become "music mad," as she expressed it, Florence found time to take lessons in the city of her birth. Singing and playing constantly, she seemed for a while to subordinate her passionate interest in nursing.

The height of her social pleasure and association with the cultured was reached when the Nightingales arrived in Paris, where they established residence for the winter. Here Florence met Mary Clark, later Madame Mohl, who became a lifelong friend of the family and visited them often. Mary was a notable figure in the intellectual circle of the capital, and at her home Florence met the distinguished guests of the season. Her hostess was brilliant and beautiful, artistic, gay, vivacious.

"Miss Clark was exceedingly kind to Florence and me," wrote Parthe, "two young girls full of all kinds of interests which she took the greatest of pains to help . . . I know now better than ever what her influence must have been to introduce an English family (two of them girls, who, if French, would not have appeared in society) into that jealously guarded sanctuary, the most exclusive aristocratic and literary salon in Paris."

Association with these brilliant people, alert to the problems of the day, stimulated Florence. She had been, until her nineteenth year, a shy country lass, but concourse with people of achievement encouraged her to be a successful conversationalist, and she became poised and confident. Her broad knowledge, gleaned from a wide acquaintance with authors living and dead, attracted the attention of even the most learned.

When spring came the Nightingales decided that the girls had received sufficient "Continental polish," and their father arranged passage for the trip home.

Apparently a life of social ease and luxurious pleasure was before Florence. Was she no longer under the spell which that persistent Voice had cast upon her? Her family believed this to be true, for they could not discern the tiny cloud now on her mental horizon—a cloud which would grow until it broke in a wild tempest.

Chapter 2

THE VISION IS BORN

AT NINETEEN Florence was an elegant rather than a beautiful girl, tall, graceful, with an expressive and mobile countenance. Her active mind lighted her face as she spoke. Her complexion was delicate, and her pensive eyes were gray. Her smile was rippled pleasingly from her lips.

Having traveled abroad and met important people, she lost her shyness, and God was preparing her soul for the work she was to accomplish by persuading politicians and statesmen, generals and privates to do her will.

"My greatest ambition was not to be remarked [observed]," she wrote concerning her younger years. "I was always in mortal fear of doing something unlike other people, and I said, 'If I were sure that nobody would remark me, I should be quite happy.' I had a morbid terror of not using my knives and forks like other people when I should come out. I was afraid to speak to children, because I was sure I should not please them."

This fear and sensitiveness indicated a hidden emotional energy which must be brought to the surface and directed into channels of active service. There were volcanoes of feeling, torrents of emotion, tempests of urges which were to be released when God's hour arrived. God's Voice was now urging Florence—educated and cultured—to devote herself to His service. As a child, she had heard the Voice and during her schooldays could not drive away the desire to become a nurse. Yet she hesitated to declare her longing.

God equipped Florence Nightingale by making her the outstanding woman of her generation, a compelling personality with an indomitable spirit and a will that would not be sidetracked. Florence could not attain this enviable position until her soul and body had become strong and mature.

Since she was six the smouldering fires of her love for nursing had remained dormant, but blazed brightly before the trip abroad in her seventeenth year, when she wrote, "God called me to His service"—nursing. As a child she believed that she belonged to God. Like Jonathan Edwards, Florence even in childhood loved God and desired to serve Him.

The religious views of Florence's father were far from conventional, but her mother was deeply pious. As a result of her mother's influence, Florence was reared in a religious atmosphere, and she did not find it difficult to hear God's call to nursing.

When ten she wrote her sister: "Dear Pop, I think of you; pray let us love one another more than we have done . . . It is the will of God, and it will comfort us in our trials through life."

A year earlier she began her journal with a sentence which was the keynote of her career: "The Lord is with thee wherever thou art." She never lost this consciousness of God's abiding presence, and many were the times when she could rely only upon it.

It was not strange that as a child she was motivated and inspired by an urge, which she interpreted to be a divine calling, to be a nurse. To Florence, life was companionship with God, and His will ruled her choices. After she had decided that God willed that she begin her nursing career, nothing could daunt her. She believed that if she obeyed God's will, He would furnish the needed soul energy, spiritual power, physical endurance and mental vigor necessary to fulfill the mission.

Said a friend, "When I look back on every time I saw her after her sixteenth year, I see that she was constantly ripening for her work . . ."

On returning from the Continent, Florence entered into the social life of her family as she had done previously. The Nightingales were extremely wealthy and found easy entrance into any social group. During the London "season" the family was in the city for the festivities. Writing to her friends abroad, she spoke intimately of the leading people of the Empire, even young Queen Victoria and her ministers, and critically she analyzed the political theories and policies of the day. She did not write of dances, dresses and sweethearts. Her letters revealed, rather, the reflections of a brilliant thinker.

When the London "season" ended, the Nightingales returned to Lea Hurst or Embley. Lea Hurst was a large mansion, having fifteen bedrooms, but Embley was even more pretentious. At both houses friends were entertained lavishly by the Nightingales, and guests came and went constantly. Anyone in trouble, sick or in need of help turned instinctively to Florence.

She was trained for the life of a socialite and lady of leisure, but she chose rather to devote herself to menial duties of service. Florence was frequently described as a "sister of mercy" or the "emergency man of the family." Indicative of her unselfish service is a letter written when her grandmother was threatened with paralysis—whom she nursed to partial recovery.

"I am very glad sometimes," she wrote a cousin, "to walk in the valley of the shadow of death, as I do here; there is something in the stillness and silence of it which levels all earthly troubles. God tempers our wings in the waters of that valley, and I have not been so happy or so thankful for a long time. And yet it is curious, in the last years of life, that we should go down hill in order to climb up on the other side; that in the struggle of the spiritual with the material part of the universe, the material should get the better and the soul just at the moment of becoming spiritualized forever should seem to become more materialized.

When a friend of Miss Clarke, her Paris acquaintance, passed away, Florence's sympathy flowed out in a letter wherein she tried to lighten the burden of grief.

"Do you think young people are so afraid of sorrow or that if they have lively spirits . . . they think these are worth anything, except in so far as they can be put at the service of sorrow, not to relieve it . . . but to sympathize with it?

"I am sure this is the one thing worth living for, and I do so believe that every tear one sheds waters some good thing into life . . .

"What nights we have had this last month, though when one thinks there are hundreds and thousands of people suffering in the same way, and when one sees in every cottage some trouble which defies sympathy, and there is all the world putting on its shoes . . . every morning all the same and the wandering earth going its inexorable treadmill through those cold-hearted stars in the eternal silence, as if nothing were the matter, death seems less dreary than life at any rate.

"The coffin of every hope is the cradle of a good experience and nobody suffers in vain."

This was the sound philosophy of suffering with which this nineteen-year-old girl fortified her life. God was to her a just and almighty Father, to whom she could turn for spiritual direction. Florence was a happy combination of a girl without a care and a woman with a future career.

She read extensively and described Carlyle's *Past and Present* as a "beautiful book." Florence commented also concerning this work, "There are bits about work. Blessed is he who has found his work; let him ask no other blessedness. He has a work, a life purpose. He has found it and will follow it." This reaction revealed her attitude.

In the light of later events, one can understand her motives. In the same letter, in which she discusses the political situation with a friend, Florence concludes, "I am going to hold my tongue and not 'meddle with politics' or 'talk about things which I do not understand.' " For a while she had toyed with the ambition of being a stateswoman, but always when other aims thrust their heads above the surface of consciousness, she submerged them speedily, for she was convinced that she would devote her life to nursing.

Many notable people encouraged and aided her projects. The Palmerstons, the Ashburtons and Dr. Fowler, who anticipated open-air treatment for the sick, were among these. A letter in which Florence describes some of these friends is not typical of the average girl in her late teens.

"Mrs. Kieth, Miss Dutton and Louisa Mackenzie may be shortly described as the respective representatives of Soul, Mind and Heart. The first one has one's whole worship, the second, one's greatest admiration and the third, one's most lively interest. Mrs. Bracebridge may be described as all three, the Human Trinity in one; and never do I see her without feeling that she is eyes to the blind and feet to the lame. Many a plan which disappointment has thinned into a phantom of my mind takes shape and fair reality when touched by her Ithuriel's spear . . ."

Florence was invited to homes where the Empire's leading figures, often the Queen herself, were present. As she mingled with them, Florence was quick to perceive the larger problems which involved various nations of the world. Describing one of these visits, she sent her cousin a lengthy description of distinguished people she had met:

"After dinner, all stood at ease about the drawing room and behaved like so many soldiers on parade. The Queen did her very best to enliven the gloom, but was at last over-powered by numbers, gagged, and had her hands tied."

But snobbishness was foreign to Florence. Although she had met distinguished people, the nation's highest and mightiest in social and political realms, she could not forget the friends about the countryside and across the channel. In an account of a social affair arranged by the Nightingales, she named some of the notable guests and then added a postscript for Miss Clark in Paris:

"Provided you come. I care for nobody, no, not I, and shall be quite satisfied."

Although Florence found it pleasant to be in the London social whirl and to converse with somber (and often dull-minded) politicians, women of high social rank, and even with the Queen, nevertheless she could not forget her ambition: to care for the sick and needy. When her mother visited afflicted and poverty-stricken families, Florence accompanied her on these benevolent and charitable missions. Mrs. Nightingale was Lady Bountiful to the needy in the vicinity of both Lea Hurst and Embley, and was an efficient organizer.

Florence wrote of her mother, "She has the genius of order, the genius to organize a parish." As she traveled with her mother, the girl gathered much helpful information concerning supervision and administration. This experience was useful in her future work and service in the Crimea.

Her heart was in work among the suffering, not in social affairs and pleasures. She was known to leave a distinguished gathering and go to the home of a sick person in the neighborhood, where she performed the most menial tasks. The country folk soon learned to love her, and her visits were eagerly awaited as those of a friend and companion, and an impersonal benefactor. She was especially welcome where there was sickness in the home, for the needy said, "She has a way about her," and this "way" was to be recognized by the nation when Florence heard the call of the wounded soldiers in the Crimea.

The clergy regarded Florence as an invaluable aid, for she organized church activities for the poor, arranged Christmas treats, and when she grew older, conducted a Bible class on Sunday afternoons in the old oratory at Lea Hurst, which had become known as the "chapel." She found more opportunity for service at Embley, which was an industrial section where the busy Arkwright and Smedley mills employed hundreds of workers, especially girls and women. Many of these lived on the Nightingale property, and Florence took a keen interest in their welfare. Several churches ministered to their spiritual needs, and the girl from the mansion gave enthusiastic aid.

Florence the God called nurse, saw little distinction between the secular tasks of visiting the sick and the spiritual duties attendant upon church activities. Into each she carried the spirit of Christ: She was a servant to those in need, whether that need was spiritual or physical. She considered nursing a divine calling, a holy task when accomplished under the directive eye of God.

Christmas was another occasion to spread cheer among the needy of village and country. Florence distributed gifts, organized entertainments for the children and planned pleasures for the poor in the workhouses. A lover of music, she trained the young people in singing, and as a result of these efforts a group of carol singers gladdened the neighborhood with their Yuletide songs.

Florence's life was busy and one would think her happy. Apparently she had all a young girl's heart could desire and would be content to spend the years in attending social functions and serving the poor. But as time passed, Florence became restless. She must heed the call of the Voice.

The call clamored for a decision. The gaiety satisfied Florence's sister, but Florence was not content with social life however glittering or social service however urgent. She must perform her work: nursing.

"What is my business in this world," she wrote during

this period, "and what have I done this last fortnight? I have read *The Daughter at Home* to Father and two chapters of Mackintosh; a volume of *Sybil* to Mamma. Paid eight visits. Done company. And that is all. They don't know how weary this way of life is to me, this table d'hote of people."

At another time the craving to begin her lifework became apparent in her writing: "My God, what is to become of me? O weary days, O evenings that never seem to end. For how many long years, I have watched that drawing-room clock and thought it would never reach the ten!" Yet when she was engaged in God's work she willingly kept all-night vigils at the bedside of some soldier in the lonely Crimea, who was begging for his mother's hand to cool his brow.

William Nightingale had nothing to engage his attention but spending fortunes which he had inherited. Consequently he made heavy tasks of the most trivial pastimes; for instance, each morning he read The London *Times* to his daughters and insisted that they listen to the lengthy tirades from the newspaper, the tedious financial notes and the social satire directed at the less favored people of the Empire. Yet he insisted that this was culturally stimulating. Florence, able to grasp a paragraph at a glance, loathed this practice, though she sat calmly through the boring sessions.

Later, however, she vented her reaction by writing, "Now, for Parthe, the morning's reading did not matter, for she went on with her drawing, but for me who had no such cover, the thing was boring to desperation . . . To be read aloud to is the most miserable exercise of the human intellect. Or rather, is it any exercise at all? It is like lying on one's back, with one's hands tied, and having liquid poured down one's throat. Worse than that, because suffocation would immediately ensue and put a stop to this senseless operation. But no suffocation would stop the other."

Occasionally she assisted with the housekeeping, and once she was left in charge of jelly-making, but this proved as dull to Florence as her father's reading of the *Times*.

"My reign is now over," she wrote a friend, after this household venture, "Though I cannot but view my fifty-six pots with the proud satisfaction"—the friend to whom she wrote was an artist—"of an artist, my head is a little on one side inspecting the happy effect of my works with more feeling of the beautiful than Parthe ever had in hers."

On another occasion she made this comment:

"I am up to my ears in linen and glass, and I am very fond of housekeeping. In this too-highly educated, too-little-active age, it at least is a practical application of our theories to do something, and yet in the middle of my lists, my green lists, my brown lists, my red lists, of all my instruments of the ornamental in culinary accomplishments which I cannot even divine the use of, I cannot help asking in my head, 'Can reasonable people want all this? Is all that china, linen, glass, necessary to make man a progressive animal?'"

These reactions reveal Florence's attitude toward routine duties, accepted by women of her day as an essential and inescapable part of life. But Florence scrutinized, analyzed. When reading the first scene of Browning's *Paracelsus*, she commented:

"Pursuing an aim to be found in life is its true misery."

She kept notebooks and under various headings, such as "Age of Reason," "Bigotry," "Creeds," "Death," and "Education," she commented on what she read and recorded her disturbing thoughts.

"I desire for a considerable time," she wrote, "to lead a life of obscurity and toil, for the purpose of allowing whatever I may have received from God to ripen, and turning it some day to the glory of His Name. Nowadays people are in too much of a hurry both to produce and consume themselves. It is only in retirement, in silence, in meditation, that are formed the men who are called to exercise an influence on society."

Florence determined to make nursing her career. In such

work she could hide herself in the cloak of obscurity and yet use her God-given talents. Often when dinner was served, Florence was conspicuously absent, and a search revealed that she was watching beside a sickbed in a humble village home. When censured by her pompous father, she explained quietly that she could not sit down to a grand dinner when she could help to assuage the pain of a friend.

"My idea of heaven," she wrote, "is when my dear Aunt Hannah and I and my boy Shore"—a member of the family of whom she was fond—"and all of us shall be together, nursing the sick people who shall be left behind, and giving each other sympathies beside, and our Saviour in the midst of us, giving us strength."

Florence's desire to be a nurse was becoming a passion, and she was growing increasingly confident that this was God's will for her life. When Julia Ward Howe and Dr. Howe visited the family at Embley, Florence told the doctor of her spiritual longing.

"If I should determine to study nursing," she asked, "and to devote my life to that profession, do you think it would be a dreadful thing?"

Her family and companions would have answered a decided "Yes," but the kindly doctor said hearteningly, "Not a dreadful thing at all. I think it would be a very good thing."

Quietly Florence made other inquiries and laid careful plans. However, she did not reveal her intentions to the members of her family, who she knew would object to such ideas, as they believed nursing to be beneath the talents of one so brilliant and well born as Florence.

One day Florence startled her parents by declaring that she planned to study nursing. On December 11, 1845, she wrote to her favorite cousin, to whom she was able to reveal the secrets of her heart.

"Well, my dearest, I have not yet come to the great thing I wanted to say," she wrote. "I have always found that

there was so much truth in the suggestion that you must dig
for hidden treasure in silence, or you will not find it; and
so I dug after my poor, little plan in silence, even from you.

"It is to go to be a nurse at Salisbury Hospital for those
few months to learn the 'prax' and then to come home and
make such wondrous intimacies at West Wellow, under the
shelter of a rhubarb powder and a dressed leg . . .

"I saw a poor woman die this summer before my eyes,
because there was no one but fools to sit up with her, who
poisoned her as much as if they had given her arsenic.

"And then I had such a fine plan for those dreadful latter
days . . . if I should outlive my immediate ties, of taking a
small house in West Wellow. Well, I do not much like talking about it, but I thought something like a Protestant sisterhood, without vows, for women of educated feelings might
be established.

"But there have been difficulties about my very first step,
which terrified Mamma. I do not mean the physically re-
volting parts of hospitals, but things about surgeons and
nurses which you may guess."

She related how a friend, Mrs. Fowler, threw cold water
upon her desire, "and nothing will be done this year at all
events." She chided her cousin with the possibility that she
would laugh at the plan, "but no one but the mother of it
knows how precious an infant idea becomes, nor how the
soul dies between the destruction of one and the taking up
of another."

Her mind was full of questions and doubts regarding her
ability to serve her Saviour, who had died for her, and this
uncertainty was reflected in her written reaction.

"I shall never do anything, and am worse than dust and
nothing. I wonder if our Saviour were to walk the earth
again, and I were to go to Him and ask whether He would
send me back to live this life again, which crushes me into

vanity and deceit. Oh, for some strong thing to sweep this loathsome life into the past."

But there were days of service ahead for Florence Nightingale. She had given birth to a brainchild which would become world renowned. She could affirm later, "I can do all things through Christ . . ."

Chapter 3

WAITING GOD'S TIME

FLORENCE KNEW where her lifework was to be found, but social barriers, family handicaps and the questionable reputation of nurses in general closed the doors to this vocation. Horrified, Florence's family threw up their hands when she told them of her desire to enter a hospital and become a nurse. They pointed to the fact that few if any positions held by women were lower from a moral standpoint than that of nursing.

Said a doctor, "Some of the nursing is done by drunken prostitutes who were given the option in the police courts of going to prison or to the hospital."

When William Nightingale heard the opinions concerning Florence's choice, he stamped his heavy foot and threatened the girl. Even those in the profession were highly critical of it. A doctor friend confided to William that "all the nurses in a certain hospital were drunkards, except two whom the surgeon could trust to give the patients their medicine." The head nurse in a London hospital told Florence, "In the course of her large experience, she had never known a nurse who was not drunken, and that there was immoral conduct

31

practiced in the very wards of which she gave me awful examples."

The Nightingale family obtained this information from another London hospital: "Drunkenness is common among the staff nurses who are chiefly of the charwoman type and frequently of bad character. The worst women we have are those who used to come in to look after the bad cases. They are the most dreadful persons."

Great was the horror which filled Mrs. Nightingale when Florence told her that she planned to enter the nursing profession, degraded by drunkards and prostitutes. The family could not tolerate such associations for their brilliant and socially successful daughter. William Nightingale knew that once Florence entered the ranks his position among the nation's elite would be ruined. He could not bear the thought that his daughter should risk lowering her virtue by observing the evil examples of which he had been told. When the girl had persuaded him to study conditions in the nursing profession, he found that without exception only the lowest class of women entered this field of service.

Some of the Nightingales' friends whispered, "Vicious and degraded patients, vicious and degraded medical students and nurses." A Brighton physician, however, had a more hopeful outlook and told William, "Women of a proper age and character are not unfit for such cases. Age, habit and office give the mind a different turn."

The prevailing opinion, however, upon which the Nightingales relied strongly, was that nursing was not a suitable task for a respectable woman, particularly one with Florence's upbringing and privileges, to say nothing of her social and financial affluence.

Florence, even though she was a conventional, sheltered, well-bred English girl, could have entered another's kitchen as a cook or a maid, but for her to become a nurse was not to be permitted.

"It was as if I wanted to be a kitchen maid," Florence

lamented, revealing the turbulence of her soul, and added poignantly, "There are private martyrs, as well as burnt and drowned ones. Society, of course, does not know them; the family cannot, because our position to one another in our families is . . . like that of the moon to the earth. The moon revolves around her, moves with her . . . yet the earth never sees but one side of her; the other side remains forever unknown."

Persuaded against her will, Florence kept her own opinion, but for the present she pigeonholed her ambition to be a nurse. She knew that the vision and the Voice were divinely given, but she did not yet have the courage to break with custom, and she lacked strength to answer the challenge.

Analyzing the reason for the drunkenness prevalent among these would-be sisters of mercy, described as prostitutes or charwomen, she decided that they drank because of overwork and insufficient food. Florence declared, "Upon an average all men and women, after a laborious day, require a good night . . . A night nurse should have food at night. In one hospital there is a rule that no night nurse is to take refreshment during her watch, the intention being to keep her more vigilantly to her duty."

Although Florence's family and convention tried to still the heavenly Voice, it continued to present the challenge. Florence was waiting God's hour when she would throw convention to the winds and prove that nurses could be as devoted as mothers and as consecrated to their holy task as sisters of mercy.

"The longer I live," she recorded in her diary, "the more I feel as if all my being was gradually drawing to one point, and if I could be permitted to return and accomplish that in another being, if I may not in this, I should need no other heaven. I could give up the hope of meeting and living with those I have loved . . . and being separated from here, if it would please God to give me, with a nearer consciousness of His presence, the task of doing this in the real life."

During this time of struggle she found a kindred spirit in Elizabeth Fry, the Quakeress who had devoted her life to bettering the condition of women prisoners. Florence found that Elizabeth's aim was similar to hers, although each worked in a different manner. Both were willing to defy convention, and tradition, to satisfy their common longing to serve humanity. Each desired to be a pioneer in her task.

Florence, considerably younger than Elizabeth, found her Quaker friend to be enthusiastic and spiritually minded. Elizabeth had visited many prisons in England and the Continent, inspected the charitable institutions, and, after coming to London, had founded a small school for training nurses. Florence questioned her friend concerning conditions prevalent at the school, and Mrs. Fry told her of the Kaiserwerth institution, founded by Pastor Kliedner, where an order of Protestant deaconesses had been instituted for the purpose of helping the sick and poor.

This was water to Florence's enthusiasm, and joyously she drank the information.

A consciousness of God's presence sustained her during this trying period. Florence met Hannah Nicholson, "Aunt Hannah" as she later called her, who was to be a spiritual aid in achieving her goal. Writing in 1843, Florence said of her friend, "An acquaintance, made with a woman to whom all unseen things seemed real and eternal things near, awakened me." Aunt Hannah did not censor nor blame the girl, but, rather, praised her ambition and sympathized with her intense desire to serve humanity. Inspiring were the spiritual messages she gave Miss Nightingale. Often she quoted Paul's words:

"Our light affliction which is but for a moment worketh for us a more exceeding and eternal weight of glory; while we look not at things which are seen; for the things which are seen are temporal, but the things which are not seen are eternal."

"Your whole life," Florence wrote to this friend, "seems

to be love, and you always find words in your heart which, without the pretension of enlightening, yet are like a clearing up to me. You always seem to rest on the heart of the divine Teacher, and to participate in His mysteries . . . Your letters stay with me when the dreams of life come one after another, clouding and covering the realities of the unseen."

Florence's correspondence with her Paris friend reveals the depths of her spiritual life. "I like those books," she wrote to Miss Clark, "where the Invisible communicates freely with the Visible Kingdom; not that they ever come up to one's idea which is always so much brighter than the execution (for the word is only the shadow cast by the light of thought) but they are suggestive."

God was preparing Florence for the struggles she was to face in the tomorrows. She must be thoroughly prepared by the blighting of her ambition to become a nurse. She must grow accustomed to meeting disappointment that later she might be able to persevere against obstacles. While her family and wealthy friends blocked her path, God was tempering her soul and developing the faith necessary for great accomplishments.

"Faith is the real ear and eye of the soul, and it would be impossible to describe the harmony and melody of music to one born deaf, or to make a blind man perceive the beauty of the effects of color, so without faith, the spiritual world is as much a hidden one to the soul as the art of painting to the blind man.

"On a dark night the moon, when at last she rises, reveals to us just at our feet, a world of objects, the presence of which we were not aware before. We see the river sparkling in the moonbeams close beside us, and the tall shadows sleeping quietly on the grass, and the sharp relief of the architectural cornices . . .

"What shall we say if one day the moon rises upon our spiritual world, and we see close at hand, ready to hold most intimate communion with us, the spirits whom we have loved and mourned as lost to us? We are like the blind man by the wayside, and ought to sit and cry, 'Lord, that we may receive our sight.'

"And when we do receive it . . . we shall perhaps find that we require no transporting into another world to become aware of the immediate presence of the Infinite Spirit . . . What we require is spiritual sight, not change of place, I believe."

Through these troublesome and dark paths she was treading, God was training Florence's soul to receive a revelation of Himself in His glorious fullness. There was a mighty mission for her to fulfill, but its accomplishment required a Spirit-filled, God-led soul. As God tempered the inner life of Moses by forty years in the Midian wilderness, and thus prepared him to lead Israel on the greatest spiritual trek of the ages, so He now sent Florence into the desert of blighted ambitions and hopes that she might lead the world to see the mighty vision which enthralled her.

"If, when the plough goes over the soul," she wrote to a friend in a particularly trying time, "there were always the hand of the Sower to scatter the seed after it, who would regret? But how often the seed-time has passed, it is too late, the harrow has gone over, the time of harvest is not."

Florence hungered. Writing to Miss Nicholson she said, "The crown of righteousness! That word always strikes me more than anything in the Bible. Strange that not happiness, not rest, not forgiveness, not glory should have been the thought of that glorious man's [Paul] mind when at the eve of the last and greatest of his labors, all desires so swallowed up in the one great craving after righteousness that, at the end of his struggles, it was mightier within him than ever, mightier even than the desire of peace."

Florence realized that efforts to better conditions in the world must be motivated by a strong love for God. At this time and later when she was deep in plans for nursing, even in the Crimea and afterward, this love for God spurred her to accomplish what others called the impossible.

"The foundation of all must be the love of God. All that I do is poisoned by the fear that I am not doing it in simplicity and godly sincerity," she declared. This girl, Florence, rich in fame and friendship, was not to be merely an ordinary nurse, but a leader of nurses, who was to open the eyes of those who believed that nursing could become a noble art, a holy career, an exalted profession. She saw human need, and realized that she must pray that others might catch the same vision.

"My sympathies are with ignorance and poverty," she observed. "My imagination is filled with the misery of this world that the only thing in which to labor that brings many returns seems to me to be helping and sympathizing there.

"All the poets sing of the glories of this world appears to me untrue; all the people I see are eaten up with poverty or disease."

The principles of work which were later to be the foundation of her success were not being developed. Life was not a round of social affairs but a treadmill of duty. "Life is no holiday game," she said, "nor a clever book, nor a school of instruction, nor a valley of tears, but it is a hard fight, a struggle, a wrestling with the principles of evil hand to hand, foot to foot. Every inch of the way must be disputed."

Keenly aware of the world's need, Florence could not be satisfied to spend her days in idle conversation with those occupied only with the superficial and squander her evenings by attending parties and gatherings of social parasites.

"The night is given us to take breath, to pray, to drink at the fountain of power, the day to use the strength which has been given us to go forth to work with till the evening."

God was delaying the launching of her work that He might inspire her with dreams of conquest and visions of victory. Florence faced a long struggle, and no weakling could achieve victory. The Almighty was preparing her soul for a lifelong battle.

She observed the idle clergy, dawdling over dogmatics, while their eyes were closed to the needs of the poor and those in prison and they said, "never a word of different plans of education, prisons, penitentiaries and so on." When her spiritual ire rose to its heights, she spoke of such men and their works as "only theology and tea mongers. It will never do unless we have a church of which the terms of membership shall be work, not doctrines."

Fires were burning in Florence's heart, volcanoes of emotion were seething, the urge to be of spiritual value to the world was growing constantly stronger. Yet the hour for the unleashing of these powers, had not yet struck. She beheld the vision, but there were trials to be endured before God was ready for her to translate this vision into action.

Outwardly life flowed on as in the past, but a revolution had taken place in Florence's heart. Her life continued to be a conventional round of jelly-making and conversations with tea-drinking friends. From Embley to London and back once more to Lea Hurst—this gaiety was broken only by nights when the heavenly Vision blazed with blending brilliance.

In London, Florence and her family listened as Jenny Lind, the famed Swedish singer, thrilled all hearers with her golden voice. Like Miss Lind, who later was to forsake the glitter of the operatic stage because it was blinding her to the glory of the Bible's truths, so Florence was to break from London society that she might become the lady whose lamp glowed upon the wounded soldiers of the Crimea.

In London she met famous people, as at Embley, and listened with admiration to the astronomers Adams and Leverrier. Among her friends were lords and their ladies, such as Sherborne and Lovelace, poets and writers, the great and the would-be great.

None of this satisfied the deep longings of Florence's

inner nature. She longed to serve in hospitals, which she often visited, and reveled in reports, which she studied carefully. Especially valuable was the annual report of Pastor Fliedner's Institution for Deaconesses, which conducted a hospital and nurses' training school. She studied this by the hour, drawing her own conclusions regarding the work, and planning possible improvements, and envisioning the growth of the endeavor.

Florence's outward compliance with convention and her inner rebellion and spiritual dissatisfaction produced a feeling of hopelessness and frustration. This conflict stole her vivacity and faded the bloom on her cheeks.

Her distraught family did not know where to turn. Psychiatry had not yet been developed, and Florence's parents were unable to administer that which would heal her sick body and disturbed soul by permitting her to enter nurse's training.

Fortunately the Bracebridges, then about to begin a tour of the Continent, came to Florence's rescue with an invitation to accompany them, and in 1847, when she was twenty-seven, they started for Rome, where they were to spend many months. The girl's one desire was to regain her health, for she sensed that if she was able to realize her ambition she must be strong physically and mentally alert.

Her father, however, considered the trip an effective method of ridding his daughter of the obsession that she wanted to become a nurse.

Florence enjoyed the trip and in the Eternal City she visited the catacombs where martyred Christians had been buried. Here she saw again the ancient churches and visited the famous galleries. William, eager to keep his daughter "under his thumb," made a list of sights to be seen and activities to be enjoyed (or endured?), and Florence methodically checked the list as she visited the places indicated by her father.

"I have had such a day," she wrote of her visit to the

Sistine Chapel, "my Golden Letter day, and of all my days in Rome, this one has been the most happy and glorious. Think of a day alone in the Sistine Chapel with Mrs. Bracebridge, quite alone, without custodians, without visitors, looking up into that heaven of angels and prophets. I did not think that I was looking at pictures, but straight into heaven itself."

She reveled in the beauties of the Sistine Chapel—and in her freedom, for at last she was beyond the control of William's will. Beholding the beauty of the famous chapel, she said, "There is Daniel, opening his window and praying to the God of his fathers three times a day, in defiance of fear." Like Daniel, she was now at last, even if for a day, free from the fear of convention, of her father's decrees, and the admonition of friends', "You must not be a nurse."

Florence's comments on the superb art reveal her spiritual exhilaration. "You see that young and noble head like an eagle's, disdaining danger, those glorious eyes undazzled by all the honors of Babylon. Then comes Isaiah. I was rather startled by finding him so young, which was not my idea of him at all. But Michelangelo knew him better. It is the perpetual youth of inspiration, the vigor and freshness, ever new, ever living, of that eternal spring of thought which is typed under that youthful face. Genius knows no age. There is security of inspiration about Isaiah. He is listening and he is speaking . . .

"I feel these things to be a part of the Word of God, of the ladder to heaven. The Word of God is all by which He reveals His thought, all by which He makes a manifestation of Himself to man."

Here also Florence met famed fellow countrymen, such as Sidney Herbert, one-time secretary of war under the mighty Peel, and discussed with him plans for bettering the living conditions of the tenants on his estate. Together they devised a plan whereby those recovering from illness should not be forced by lack of means or accommodations to return to work immediately, but should be sent to a convalescent home or cottage hospital where they could recuperate.

Hearing of the philanthropic work accomplished by a convent, Florence met the Lady Superior, for whom she formed a warm attachment, and through whom she made a thorough study of the organization. The convent also conducted a school for girls and an orphanage, and for ten days Florence went into retreat. At the close of this period she reached the conclusion that whatever the form of her future training should take, if and when she had a school for nurses, devotion must become a part of the training. She was convinced that spiritual strength plus training qualified a girl to become a healer of the sick.

Returning home in the spring of 1848, she resumed, to her family's delight, the round of social duties. While in London for the season she met Lord and Lady Ashley, later to become Lord Shaftesbury, and through them learned of the Ragged School work. Here she caught the gleam of the possibilities which training would open for nurses. This, however, did not satisfy her, for she wrote Madame Mohl, "In London there has been the usual amount of charity balls, charity concerts, charity bazaars, whereby people bamboozle their consciences and shut their eyes."

She managed, however, to break away from this social "bamboozlement" to visit the hospitals and to work in the Ragged Schools. The more she saw of such sacrificial living, the stronger grew her distaste for the luxuries and trivialities of her own existence.

"Ought not one's externals," she entered in her diary under date of July 2, 1849, "to be as nearly as possible an incarnation of what life really is? Life is not a green pasture and a still water, as our homes make it. Life is to some, forty days' fasting, moral or physical, in the wilderness; to some, it is fainting under the carrying of the cross; to some, it is crucifixion; to all, a struggle for truth, for safety.

"Life is seen in a much truer form in London than in the

country. In an English country place, everything that is
painful is so carefully removed out of sight behind those
fine trees, to a village three miles off. In London, at all
events, if you open your eyes, you cannot help seeing in the
next street that life is not as it has been made to you. You
cannot get out of a carriage at a party without seeing what
is in the faces making the lane on either side, and without
feeling tempted to rush back and say, 'These are my brothers
and sisters.' "

If free to follow her inclination, Florence would have
rushed from that party and found an old sick and forsaken
woman in the slums whom she would have gladly nursed back
to health. "But it would never do for a young woman of
your station in life to go out in London without a servant"—
thus Florence's father sought to subdue her longings.

Meanwhile the caged eagle beat its wings upon bars. The
family was moved by her distress but unwilling to relieve
the source of tension. The Bracebridges planned to winter
in Egypt and invited Florence to join them. Florence's
parents consented, hopeful that the visit would accomplish
what the trip to Rome had failed to achieve—to remove
from the girl's mind the foolish notions with which she was
obsessed.

Chapter 4

DONNING THE NURSE'S UNIFORM

To FLORENCE, Egypt was a land of delight, and her keen mind found much to employ it. Eagerly she studied dynasties, copies plans of temples and analyzed Egyptian mythology. She was puzzled constantly, however, by the solemnity of the land and its inhabitants.

"Nothing ever laughs or plays. Everything is grown up and grown old," she wrote, after charting, checking and observing. A lover of beauty, she saw enchanting pictures in the shadowy temples and the sand that glittered in the sun.

"I thought of the worshipers three thousand years ago," she said, "how they by this time have reached the goal of spiritual ambition . . . how we stand there with the same goal before us, only as distant as a star, but as sure and fixed."

She could not wrest her mind from the vexing problems presented by the poverty and sickness of the people, and she wrote a friend, "If I were a Pharaoh now, I would choose the Arab form and come back to help these poor people." Writing to her family, she speaks of "poking my nose into all the villages and seeing for myself how these poor people live. They call me the wild ass of the wilderness, snuffing up the wind, because I am so fond of getting away."

These rambling tours throughout the land were to continue until April, 1850, when the party went to Athens, where Florence was to meet a new situation, study a new group of myths and enjoy scenery entirely different from the wild Cairo country. One of the most enjoyable experiences of the visit was the meeting with two American missionaries, the Hills, who conducted a school and orphanage in Athens. The Missionary school was conducted by a Greek refugee whose life had been full of tragic adventure.

"How worthless my life seems to be by the side of these women," Florence recorded in her diary. The scenes of beauty, the glories of ancient Greek art and sculpture—these became insignificant beside the orphanage and mission school. Hers was a gilded, a wasted life.

In the background of her mind was a desire to visit Kaiserwerth in Germany, a desire which was to be fulfilled on this journey. On July 31 she arrived at the scene of Pastor Fliedner's work, of which she says, "I could hardly believe I was there. With the feeling with which a pilgrim first looks on the Kedron, I saw the Rhine, dearer to me than the Nile."

Kaiserwerth was founded by Theodore Fliedner, who was the son and grandson of Lutheran clergymen and himself a minister. Born in 1800 at Epstein, a small village on the Rhine, he at twenty-two was called to pastor the Protestant church at Kaiserwerth, on the Rhine near Dusseldorf. The closing of the mill brought difficult days to the community and sent the pastor into Holland, England and his native Germany to seek funds for his impoverished people. In England he met Florence's friend, Elizabeth Fry, who interested him in prison reform. On returning to Kaiserwerth, he entered prison work at near-by Dusseldorf and decided to study and solve the problem of discharged prisoners.

As Florence visited his village, he pointed out the old building which he had repaired in 1833 and made habitable for the prisoners who came here after having been discharged. This, he said, was the beginning of the Kaiserwerth Institution, which eventually consisted of an orphanage, an infant school—many prisoners had children to be cared for —a hospital in which to train volunteer nurses as deaconesses and a training school for teachers.

The work nearest his heart was the hospital, for, like his visitor, he had been moved with compassion for the sick. The poverty and distress of the villagers caused him on October 14, 1846, to use the old dilapidated mill which had ruined the prosperity of the community. Here with only six sheets but patients a-plenty he had opened his hospital, and when Florence visited the institution, boasted a hundred beds and one hundred and sixteen nursing deaconesses who were being trained while many others were engaged in the work elsewhere.

Florence resolved with new determination to become a nurse, and she made this significant entry in her diary: "Left Kaiserwerth feeling so brave, as if nothing could ever vex me again."

Returning home, she was forced again into the social treadmill. Although she did not want to injure the family further, she began to wonder if the obstacles, "mountains of difficulties," as she called them, which blocked her path were not man-made rather than God-willed. Until now she had thought of them as a cross to bear—a cross sent by God. Henceforth she began to view them rather as an obstacle to be overcome, so she started to pray for grace and strength to conquer them.

"I must take some things," she recorded in her diary on June 8, 1851, "as few as I can, to enable me to live. I must take them—they will not be given me—take them in a true spirit of doing Thy will, not of snatching them for my will."

The resolve to do God's will and ennoble the nursing profession was becoming constantly stronger, but she now encountered a new problem. Until now she had thought nothing, at least little, of marriage. Her friends, and espe-cially her parents, had "longed for some noble-hearted, true man, one who can love her as she deserved to be loved," to establish Florence in her own home.

With the ingenuity of marriage brokers, they presented possible suitors to their thirty-year-old daughter. One by one they came. Some elegantly stated their suits; some tried vigorously to persuade Florence of their true love; others conducted their courtship without enthusiasm. The girl's heart nearly yielded to the pressure of their attentions, but she wrote in her diary concerning one candidate:

"I have an intellectual nature that requires satisfaction and that I could find in him. I have a passional nature which requires satisfaction and that I could find in him. I have a moral, an active, nature which requires satisfaction that would not find it in his life. I can hardly find satis-faction of any of my natures. Sometimes I think I will satisfy my passional nature at all events, because that will at least secure me from the evil of dreaming."

Pausing for a moment to examine the subject in the light of her past, she asked, "But would it? I could be satisfied to spend a life with him combining our different powers in some great object. I could not satisfy this nature by spend-ing a life with him in making society and arranging do-mestic things . . .

"To be nailed to a continuation and exaggeration of my present life without hope of another would be intolerable to me. Voluntarily to put it out of my power ever to be able to seize the chance of forming for myself a true and rich life would seem to me like suicide."

This was Florence's final word concerning the gentleman in question. She did, however, long for a true mate, and wrote of this desire: "Marrying a man of high and good purpose, and following out that purpose with him, is the happiest lot . . . The highest, the only true love is when two persons, a man and a woman, who have an attraction for each other, unite together in some true purpose for mankind and God . . . that these two when the right two are united shall throw themselves fearlessly into the universe and do its work, secure of companionship and sympathy."

She entertained other thoughts on the subject also, and when she saw single women who were blessed in their activities, she said, "I think Providence has as clearly marked out some to be single women as He has others to be wives . . . I think some have every reason for not marrying . . . There are women of intellectual or actively moral natures for whom marriage (unless it realizes the perfect ideal) means the sacrifice of their higher capacities to the satisfaction of their lovers."

This battle of ideas, begun by her parents' desire to subdue her passion for nursing, was ended on her thirtieth birthday, when she wrote in her diary the final word:

"I am thirty, the age at which Christ began His mission. Now, no more childish things, no more vain things, no more love, no more marriage. Now, Lord, let me think only of Thy will."

This was the vision to which henceforth she was to be true; this was her goal. She sought not only to be of service in the field of nursing but she was convinced that God wanted her "to strive after a better life for women"— to free them from the confines of what had until now been their only sphere of service: the home. She was willing to fight that women might be free to enter other occupations, and realms of service as God called and enabled them, professions which until now had been open only to men.

Florence could not be content to destroy the flame of enthusiasm, to lose the vision God had given her. There were goals to be attained—goals which social pressure must not destroy.

"A woman cannot live in the light of intellect," she wrote concerning her struggle to free not only herself but women in general for divine service. "Society forbids it. Those conventional frivolities which are called her duties forbid it. Her domestic duties, high sounding words which for the most part are bad habits . . . forbid it. What are these duties (or bad habits)? Answering a multitude of letters, which lead to nothing, from her so-called friends; keeping herself up to the level of the world that she may furnish her quota of amusement at the breakfast table; driving out her company in the carriage."

This, of course, was the life of the idle-rich woman, to which Florence had been accustomed, and from this she longed to be free to invest her talents in the calling which God had given her. "Women never have a half-hour in all their lives . . . that they can call their own, without fear of offending or hurting someone . . . A woman could never get anything but odd moments to herself. Can we fancy Michelangelo running up and putting a touch to his Sistine ceiling in odd moments?"

Meanwhile she mulled over the plans for the work she hoped to do and considered various methods of collecting funds, either to found a hospital or establish a sisterhood of nurses. She reached the conclusion that she needed training. Good intentions were not sufficient; she must have experience with which to build.

The opportunity came from an unexpected source. The illness of Florence's sister caused William Nightingale to send his daughter to Carlsbad on the Continent. Taking a new attitude toward obstacles, Florence announced that while Parthe and her mother were at Carlsbad, she would go to Kaiserwerth for training.

"What will people say!" her mother exclaimed. But what people said or thought meant little or nothing to Florence, and she determined to enter the school at Kaiserwerth.

In July, 1851, during her thirty-first year, the dream she had cherished for more than twenty years reached fulfillment and she entered the Fliedner school in Germany, where she stayed until October of that year. She donned for

the first time the blue cotton dress, the white apron and
the muslin cap worn by those in training.

She was not seeking ease, and when the pastor tested
her mettle by suggesting, "You won't want to scrub that
dirty floor," she gave him a quizzical glance, got soap and
water and scrubbed the place thoroughly. "It was a dirty
floor, too," said one of the deaconesses.

Florence did both day and night nursing, and though
she came primarily for this nurse's training, she entered
eagerly into all the work of the institution. She hoped that
God would enable her to establish such a home and training
center in England. She accompanied Frau Fliedner upon
her rounds of district visiting, and every part of the welfare
work came under her keen and critical eye. The long hours
and poor food did not add to the physical enjoyment of the
rigorous duties.

"The world here fills life with interest and strengthens
me in body and mind," she wrote her mother. "Until yesterday I never had time even to send my things to the wash.
We have ten minutes for each of our meals, of which we have
four. We get up at five, breakfast one half hour before six.

"The patients dine at eleven; the sisters at twelve. We
drink tea (i.e., a drink made of ground rye) between two
and three and sup at seven. We have two ryes and two
broths, ryes at six and three, broths at twelve and seven,
bread at the two former, vegetables at twelve. Several evenings in the week, we collect in the great hall for Bible lessons
. . . The man's wisdom and knowledge of human nature is
wonderful.

"This is life. Now I know what it is to love life."

This was the life for which Florence had pined during
the years since God gave her the vision of the sick and needy.
Gladly she relinquished romance that she might serve others.

Happy in her works, she was nevertheless saddened by her
mother's disapproval of it. She craved sympathy and sought
understanding, especially from her family—for at heart she

was a Nightingale, wealthy, cultured, the possessor of a
rich social background. However, only her father gave her
the understanding for which she longed.

"I should be happy here as the day is long," she wrote
her mother, "if I could hope that I had your smile, your
blessing, your sympathy upon it, without which I cannot be
quite happy. My beloved people, I cannot bear to grieve you.
Life and everything in it that charms you, you would sacrifice for me; but unknown to you is my thirst, unseen by you
are the waters which would save me.

"To save me, I know, would be to bless yourselves,
whose love for me passes the love of woman . . . Give me
time. Trust me, help me. Say to me, 'Follow the dictates of
that spirit within thee.' Oh, my beloved people, that spirit
shall never lead me to anything unworthy of one who is
yours to love."

The conflict continued to rage in her soul——the conflict
between love for her family and the desire to answer God's
call, which she knew she must follow at all costs, even if
she lost the support of her loved ones.

Happy in her work and eager to learn all she could
about it, she saw flaws in the pastor's procedures. "The
nursing is nil," she said, "the hygiene terrible. The hospital
is certainly the worst part of Kaiserwerth. I took all the
training that was to be had there, for there was none to be
had in England, but Kaiserwerth was far from having
trained me."

In contrast, however, she found the "tone of the work
wonderful." She declared that the pastor's addresses were
the best she had ever heard, and she described life at the
institution as "a better life for woman, a scope for the
exercises of morally achieving powers." She viewed the
practical training in the "service of man as the service of
God" and believed that the pastor was helping women to
achieve a spiritual independence which they had never
known. This work combined her two major aims: practical

nurse's training and an opportunity to achieve a freer and larger life for women in general. She realized, however, that she was merely glimpsing the Promised Land.

Returning to England with the family in October, she was spiritually at rest for the inner conflict had nearly ceased as the result of the time spent at the pastor's institution. At this time she met George Eliot, who said of her, "I was much pleased with her. There is a loftiness of mind about her which is well expressed by her form and manner." Elizabeth Barrett Browning characterized Florence by saying, "I remember her face and her graceful manner and the flowers she sent me afterward. She is an earnest, noble woman."

Florence was not content to resume domestic duties, but sought to continue her training by visiting hospitals in Ireland and elsewhere. She expressed her conclusions in a manuscript which disclosed the workingman's belief in God or, rather, the lack of religious emphasis in the training of workers.

Finally she obtained her parents' consent to study nursing under the supervision of a Catholic sisterhood in Paris and while there to inspect Parisian hospitals. Accordingly she left for Paris on February 3, 1853. Before taking up her duties she inspected hospitals and infirmaries. She was especially delighted to see women surgeons in action. When about to enter training, however, she was called to England because of her grandmother's illness.

On returning home she was asked to become the superintendent of an institution which had been established to care for "gentlewomen," as they were then known, during illness. She finally accepted the position, but only after the usual discussions and arguments with her family, but she emerged victorious. The institution had been established a few years previous to aid and give medical assistance to governesses and other gentlewomen of limited means, but had not proved a successful venture. When Florence was placed in charge of the project a new house was purchased on Harley Street in London.

"Harley Street," she wrote a friend, "is a sanitarium for the sick governesses, managed by a committee of fine ladies. I am to have the choosing of the house, the appointment of the chaplain and the government of the funds, as those of the committee are at present minded. But Isaiah himself could not prophesy how they will be minded at eight o'clock this evening."

Ten days later she had her first tiff with the good ladies, about which she wrote to her Parisian friend, Madame Mohl, "I have been in service for ten days and have had to furnish an entirely empty house in that time. My committee refused to take in Catholic patients whereupon I wished them good morning, unless I might take in Jews and their rabbis. So now it is settled that we are to take in all denominations whatever and allow them to be visited by their priests and muftis, provided I will receive the obnoxious animal at the door . . . and bring him downstairs again in a noose out to the street. Amen! From philanthropy and all deceits, good Lord, deliver us."

Here Florence learned a lesson she was to remember throughout life. Later she was often described as "the woman who ought to have been a general or a diplomat." She tells us how she received her training in the art of diplomacy. Once when the committee of women was obstreperous, she drew up a series of five resolutions which she declared to be the work of physicians.

"When I entered here, I determined I would never intrigue. Now I perceive I do all my business by intrigue . . . I executed a series of resolutions on five subjects and presented them as coming from medical men. I proposed and carried them in committee without telling them that they came from me and not from the medical men; and then, and not till then, I showed them to the medical men without telling them that they were already passed in committee.

Success is said to make an insurrection into a revolution . . .

"The medical men approved them all and thought they were their own."

Untiring in her labors, she was successful in managing the home, where she supervised nursing, housekeeping and matters of finance. She was able to reduce the operating expenses by almost half, and for the first time in her life she was thoroughly content. Of the break with her family she said, "It is with the deepest consideration and the fullest advice that I have taken the step of leaving home, and it is a *fait accompli*."

Success crowned her Harley Street labors and she was asked to become the superintendent of nurses at famous King's College Hospital. When her heart was set upon this new task, early one fall morning in 1854, while reading the *Times,* she discovered a dispatch from William Howard Russell, a front-line correspondent in the Crimean War which had startled England a short time before. These significant words were to be used of God to lead her into His will.

"It is with feelings of surprise and anger," said the correspondent, "that the public will learn that no sufficient preparations have been made for the proper care of the wounded. Not only are there no dressers and nurses . . . but there is not even linen to make bandages for the wounded . . . There is no preparation for the commonest surgical operations. Not only are the men kept in some cases for a week without the hand of a medical man coming near the wounds, not only are they left to expire in agony, unheeded and shaken off, though catching desperately to the surgeon whenever he makes his rounds . . . but it is found . . . that the men must die through the medical staff of the British Army having forgotten that old rags are necessary for the dressing of wounds . . ."

Florence's eyes grew misty as she read. Her heart was stirred by the writer's challenge to the nation, ". . . are there no devoted women amongst us able and willing to go forth to minister to the sick and suffering soldiers of the East in the hospitals at Scutari? Are none of the daughters of England, at this extreme hour of need, ready for such a work of mercy?"

This was Florence's hour—the hour for which she had been mentally and spiritually prepared for twenty years. Now she was familiar with hospitals and had received what nurse's training was available. The good women on her Harley Street committee had given her excellent training in tact and diplomacy. God was speaking in clarion tones, and Florence was ready to rise and answer the correspondent's challenge:

"Yes, there is a devoted woman amongst us, able and willing to go forth to minister to the sick soldiers at Scutari. Here am I, Lord, send me!"

The tortuous path that had been blocked with difficulties suddenly became a great highway—the highway of holiness of which Isaiah spoke so beautifully—the highway of "service of men organized as the service of God." She was ready to march on this highway. For this hour she had prepared, and for this moment she had prayed.

Chapter 5

GOD'S NURSE IN THE CRIMEA

FLORENCE SAT in a daze as she read the challenging newspaper account. She was an Englishwoman, trained for the task, and immediately she faced this question, *Has God prepared me for such an emergency?* They were dying out there in the Crimea—those fair sons of England—and could she do less than help them in their dying hour?

She read further of the war with Russia which had broken out in the spring of 1854, and by October, news of the Alma victory had made the nation rejoice. The concensus was that the war would soon be over, and the newspapers shared this belief. But Florence was stunned by Russell's declaration that the sick and dying were being neglected. Reports from the battlefronts began to pour in and she read them with disgust, disgust which became fury.

"You cannot imagine anything so fearful as the condition of the wounded soldiers here," said one writing from the field of battle. "There are three thousand lying in the barracks and not even doctors to take care of them and no nurses . . . You will understand better the state of these poor creatures when I tell you that many of them were brought down here three days after the battle without their wounds having been washed even. And most of them that have died since have done so after the amputations from the want of proper care."

Florence's mind revolted at the thought of living in ease when such conditions as these prevailed. She had prayed to be a nurse, sought an opening, and here was a field of service where her talents could be used.

"The ship (bringing the wounded to Scutari)," she read further, "was literally covered with prostrate forms . . . The officers could not get below to find their sextants and the run was made at hazards. The worst cases were placed on the upper deck which in a day or two became a mass of putridity. The neglected gunshot wounds bred maggots which crawled in every direction, infecting the food. The putrid animal matter caused such a stench that the officers and crew were nearly overcome, and the captain is now ill from the effects of misery. All blankets (1,500) have been thrown overboard as useless."

The shouting and the tumult of victory died and a clamor for help took its place. Throughout the nation committees were organized to help the wounded soldiers at Scutari. Money was subscribed and organizations offered their services. But the call for a leader became louder, and as she sat in her nurse's room at the hospital, Florence heard not only the nation's challenge but also God's call to the task. Nor was she disobedient to the heavenly vision, and within two days had made her plans to go.

Throughout the land the name of Florence Nightingale was on people's tongues as the leader, the chief nurse, for the barracks. Henry E. Manning, later Cardinal Manning, knew Florence and suggested that she assume leadership. Lady Forester subscribed a thousand dollars for the project and suggested that Florence be selected to fill the position.

Florence, actively interested in the appointment, wrote to Sidney Herbert, then Minister of War (she later learned that he had written her at the same time): "A small private expedition of nurses has been organized for Scutari, and I have been asked to command it." In the letter, sent to Lady Herbert, since her husband was out of London at the time, Florence opened her heart. She said that the nurses were ready to sail, and she sought his official sanction.

"What does Mr. Herbert say to the scheme?" she continued. "Does he think it will be objected to by the authorities? Would he give us any advice or letters of recommendation? And are there any stores for the hospital he would advise us to take out?"

She informed the Minister of War that she was leaving on the following Tuesday and planned to catch the Marseilles boat for Constantinople, "where I leave my nurses, thinking the medical staff at Scutari will be more frightened than amused at being bombarded by a parcel of women, and I cross over to Scutari with someone from the Embassy to present my credentials and put ourselves at the disposal of the doctors."

She asked that Lady Herbert or a member of her committee write a letter of recommendation setting forth her qualifications for the task involved. She wanted her to declare, "This is not a lady but a real hospital nurse . . . And she has had experience . . ."

Although the Minister of War was out of the city and did not receive the letter immediately, he wrote Florence at the same time, and stated in this letter:

"There is but one person in England that I know of who would be capable of organizing and superintending such a scheme, and I have been several times on the point of asking you hypothetically if, supposing the attempt were made, you would undertake to direct it.

"The selection of the rank and file of nurses will be very difficult . . . The difficulty of finding women equal to a task, after all, full of horrors, and requiring, besides knowledge and good will, great energy and great courage, will be great. The task of ruling them and introducing system among them, great, and not the least will be the difficulty of making the whole work smoothly with the medical authorities out there."

Coming directly to the point, he asked Florence if she would listen to "the request to go and superintend the whole thing." He added, "Upon your decision will depend the ultimate success or failure of the plan. Your own qualities, your knowledge and your power of administration . . . your rank and position in society give you advantage in such a work which no other person possesses."

Florence was working primarily to establish a field for women in such crises, and the Minister of War believed that "if this succeeds, an enormous amount of good will be done . . . and a prejudice will have been broken through and a precedent established which will multiply the good to all time."

When Florence suggested the plan to her parents, they at once gave their consent, for they had changed their attitude toward the career she had outlined for herself. Parthe said, "The government has asked, I should say entreated, Flo to go out and help in the hospital at Scutari. I am sure you will feel that it is a great and noble work, and that it is a real duty, for there is no one . . . I believe truly, who has the knowledge and zeal necessary to make such a step succeed . . . I must say the way in which all things have tended to and fitted her for this is so very remarkable that one cannot but believe she was intended for it."

This conception of Flo's work differed markedly from that which the family had previously held. Parthe was right, she was intended, God-intended, for this work. It was a divine call, a divine preparation, a divine leadership for this emergency. God's hour had struck and Florence was ready.

In five days she had made preparations to leave, yet she

remained calm, unruffled, efficient. Parthe presents this description:

"She is as calm and composed in all this furious haste, with the War Office, the Military Medical Board, half the nurses in London to speak to, her own committee and institution, as if she were going for a walk." A friend described her at the time by saying, "She has such nerve and skill and is so wise and quiet. Even now she is in no bustle or hurry, though so much is on her hands and so many people volunteering their services."

Applicants volunteered by the scores, and came from all classes and conditions of life. "I wish," wrote Mary Stanley, a bishop's daughter, "all who hereafter may complain of the women selected could have seen the set we had to choose from. All London was scoured. We felt ashamed to have in the house such as came; one alone expressed a wish to go from any good motive. Money was the only inducement."

This problem had been forseen by Florence, and she had likewise anticipated the supervisory difficulty. Hence she thought it advisable to limit the number to twenty. But the Minister of War overruled her and selected forty as the number. Thirty-eight women were eventually selected. Other difficulties arose. The church groups urged that representation be restricted to those within their circles, but said there must be no religious discrimination. The Low Church objected to her accepting High Anglicans or Roman Catholics for this service.

Desiring to secure trained women, Florence had applied to the Protestant Institute for Nurses and to the High Church, St. John's House. Some of these groups objected to the fact that the nurses were to be under the control of one woman, especially Florence Nightingale. During this period of denominational bickering and sectarian quibbling a wise clergyman remarked:

"Miss Nightingale belongs to a sect which unfortunately is a very rare one: the sect of the Good Samaritan."

The military problem became vexing, for the introduction of women into military hospitals was an experiment against which the hard-shell traditions of England were set as precedents. Said a military leader, sarcastically expostulating against the plan, "Women will be wanting to teach us to fight next."

Florence, always a red-tape cutter and able to leap to the heart of a problem, insisted and rightly that all matters pertaining to her part of the venture should be in her hands. She knew something of the difficulties which arose when authority was delegated to a half-dozen groups or committees or heads of departments. Sir Herbert, knowing well Florence's qualification for the task, took it upon himself to secure such authority for her. Consequently she was officially appointed by the Government as Superintendent of Female Nursing Establishment in the English General Military Hospital in Turkey. Florence was able to bear the pretentious title with humility. To her this simply meant bringing the care of trained and efficient nurses to the wounded at Scutari. She determined to execute the task faithfully, regardless of difficulties or routine.

This unprecedented action by the Government in appointing a woman to this high position caused much inquiry regarding Florence Nightingale and why she had received the favor. In England it was considered improper for a woman to nurse in a military hospital, and prevailing opinion was that women were entirely too ignorant of such work to undertake it and too frail physically to endure the strain. The newspapers, however, came to Florence's rescue and told of her social position, education and accomplishments.

"Miss Nightingale is one of those whom God formed for

great ends," said an editorial. "You cannot hear her say a few sentences, no, not even look at her, without feeling that she is an extraordinary being. Simple, intellectual, sweet, full of love and benevolence, she is a fascinating and perfect woman. She is tall and pale. Her face is exceedingly lovely; but better than all is the soul's glory that shines through every feature. Nothing can be sweeter than her smile. It is like a sunny day in summer."

When the day of departure arrived, Florence received many letters from friends, two of which touched her deeply. Said Sir Henry E. Manning, "God will keep you, and my prayer for you will be that your one Object of worship, Pattern of imitation and Source of consolation and strength may be the sacred heart of our Divine Lord." The other was from the man she had loved but left for the work that meant more to her than all else.

"I hear you are going to the East," he wrote. "I am happy it is so, for the good you will do there and I hope you will find some satisfaction in it yourself. I cannot forget how you went to the East once before, and here am I writing quietly to you about what you are going to do now. You can undertake that when you could not undertake me. God bless you, dear friend, wherever you go."

After Florence's death, this letter was found among her precious keepsakes. It must have made her, as she sailed on this mission of love and service, both sad and happy . . . sad to leave a noble friend, happy that she could lose herself in a glorious mission.

In addition to the thirty-eight nurses were Mr. and Mrs. Bracebridge, old friends with whom she had traveled much, a courier and a clergyman. Samuel Smith, Florence's uncle, accompanied the party as far as Marseilles. The group, journeying through France, were received with acclaim, for France was an ally of England in the war. Porters, hotel attendants and all those who served the travelers refused to accept pay. Those with loved ones at the front thronged them trying to get word to Florence about son, sweetheart or husband.

Many times Miss Nightingale heard the words, "My Pierre —if you should see him—a fine boy . . ." "A handsome man, my husband, always with a smile. Tell him . . ." The broken sentences poured out the love of the sender for the soldier far from home. These messages revealed the torn souls of the women who were suffering at home.

"Still very hard work for Flo," wrote the uncle about the trip, "to keep forty in good humor. Arranging the rooms of five different sets each night before sitting down to supper took a long time, and then calling all to be down at six ready to start. She bears all wonderfully, so calm, winning everybody . . . Where she was seen or heard, there was nothing but admiration from high and low. Her calm dignity influenced everybody. I am sure the nurses quite love her already."

In another letter he says, speaking of the crowds who thronged the party, "shopkeepers, visitors, nurses, servants, every minute. There she was receiving the Inspector-General, the Consul and Agent, the Queen's Messenger, *Times'* correspondent, and two or three shopkeepers with the same serenity as if in a drawing room. The rough hospital nurses after breakfasting and dining with us and receiving all her attention were quite humanized. 'We never had so much care taken of our comforts before,' they said. 'We had no notion Miss Nightingale would slave herself for us.'"

This slaving was Flo's happiness. She was a follower of the Good Samaritan and found happiness only in giving herself freely to all in need. It was this unselfish spirit which prompted her to offer her life on the altar of sacrifice that others might be healed.

Upon reaching Marseilles, with wise forethought and against the advice of the Army Medical Department, she provided at her own expense numerous supplies, such as beds, medical equipment and food. Florence's womanly intuition and practical sense had told her to do so. Although totally unacquainted with army hospital work, nevertheless she knew human nature, and was quick to anticipate future needs. Later events proved her wisdom and efficiency.

The trip to Constantinople on the *Vectis* was rough, and when this band of women nurses, the first to sail on a similar mission, reached port on November 4, 1854, they were in poor physical condition. Much was ahead of them, for they arrived the day before the terrible battle of Inkerman and ten days before the more serious battle of Balaclava, when they were to receive their bloody initiation.

"At six o'clock yesterday," said Florence in a letter home, "I staggered on deck to look at the plains of Troy, the tomb of Achilles, the little harbor of Tenedos, between which and the main shore our *Vectis* with stewards' cabins and galley torn away, creaking, shrieking, storming, rushed on the way . . . Reached Constantinople this morning in a thick and heavy rain. Bad news from Balaclava. The wounded are, I believe, to be placed in our care. They are landing them now."

On the eight-day trip from the French port she had, in addition to providing for the comfort of her nurses, been contemplating the work ahead and weaving a network of plans to cover foreseen and unknown eventualities. But she little dreamed what awaited her—blood, the cries of the dying, the moans of the wounded.

Florence knew that during the Crimean War the principal British hospitals were located at Scutari or in its immediate vicinity and numbered four: the General Hospital, the Barrack Hospital, the Palace Hospital and, several miles distant at Koulali, a group of buildings used as hospitals or wounded sheds. The gallant woman and her party of nurses left immediately for the Barrack Hospital, which she found to be beautifully situated—if such a blood-drenched scene as this could be called beautiful—on a slope which permitted a view of the Marmora Sea and the Bosphorus. She characterized it as "the most beautiful view in the world," though she had no time to enjoy the setting.

The nurses occupied as little room as possible so as to provide the maximum space for the wounded. The women's quarters were hence uncomfortable and cramped. Florence placed thirteen in one small room, eight in another and ten in the third. At one time her own camp bedstead was behind a screen in the kitchen, so willing was she to accept the hardships which her fellow nurses endured.

"Occasionally our roof is torn off," she wrote, "or the windows are blown in, and we are under water for the night."

Her first task, after the nurses had been cared for, was to make an inspection trip, which enabled her to discover the terrible conditions in which the wounded men were living or dying. She found under the hospital sewers loaded with filth and the corridors and wards reeked with the stench.

There were few if any hospital comforts and necessities, nor were there sufficient beds on which to lay the wounded. Mattresses were hastily stuffed with whatever was available, and thrown on the floors where the wounded were placed. Basins, towels, soap, brooms, knives, forks and clean linen were lacking.

The ventilation defied description. "Dwelling in the worst part of the large cities of Europe which I have visited furnish their crowded inmates with better air," Florence later told an investigating committee.

She found the men lying in their uniforms, stiff with blood, covered with filth, their hair blood-matted. Maggots crawled over them. The sheets, made of course canvas, were so rough that the wounded begged the nurses and doctors to leave them in their blood-soaked blankets. There was no furniture. Empty beer or wine bottles served as candlesticks.

When Florence inspected the food supplies, she revolted at the thought that these wounded men had to eat the heavy boiled or fried foods or go without, which many were forced to do.

Looking outside a sickroom window, Florence saw a pile of amputated arms and legs which had been hurled from the operating room. From another window she saw six decomposed dogs, rotted beyond recognition. These gruesome sights could be easily observed by the miserable patients. Fifty per cent of the men were lying in rags, their shirts—if they were fortunate enough to have them—saturated with blood.

These were but a few of the appalling conditions which faced Florence Nightingale. In fact, there was little worthy of the British Empire, for everywhere the valiant nurse observed disorder, confusion and a lack of management which bordered on dishonesty. Walking the corridors, she saw that the wounded were in all available beds, on the floors, in the corridors, in fact everywhere, and "those from Balaclava were being brought in."

The task confronting her seemed to require superhuman strength, but with a firm faith in her mighty God she undertook it. These conditions, she avowed, must be remedied; the thousands of wounded must be cared for. Florence realized that if she and her forty nurses did not bring order out of this chaos—the task challenged five hundred nurses—and did not give the men the care they needed, the entire venture would be a failure, and the world would lose its faith in women as nurses at the battlefront hospitals.

She prayed for strength that the venture might not fail, and while praying, she rolled up her sleeves and devised a system for nursing the wounded, her immediate task. Meanwhile, however, she considered possible methods of eliminating the terrible conditions and appalling sights. She knew that the people at home, in government circles and other spheres of society, must be made to realize the cause of such conditions and to demand their correction.

Chapter 6

"THE LADY WITH THE LAMP"

FLORENCE HAD NO TIME for a rest between arriving and taking up her work, for around her was the wreckage of the battlefield. Within twenty-four hours after she landed, the battle of Inkerman spawned its hundreds of wounded soldiers into the hospitals. Five hundred arrived at one time only thirty minutes after notice of their coming had been received. These added to the more than a thousand patients under her immediate care demanded all her reserve energy.

Over rough seas the cruel Turks had brought the five-hundred boatloads of patients, their clothing stiff with blood, their wounds gaping, their broken bones unset. Many of the men were shirtless, their clothes having been torn off by those who had served as stretcher-bearers. Florence directed that mattresses should be placed everywhere—on the floor, in the corridors, wherever there was space.

"We have four miles of beds," she wrote, "eighteen inches apart. We are steeped to our necks in blood. The wounded are now lying up to our very door. And there are two more ships loading at the Crimea with wounded."

In eight hours the men were washed, made as comfortable as possible, and four hundred were given the thrill of wearing clean shirts which had been generously provided by the agent of the London *Times* fund. Within ten days she had already, despite the constant care of the newly wounded, equipped two diet kitchens in different parts of the building and had placed three boilers on a staircase to furnish the men with more palatable food than they had received. Previous to this time large copper kettles had been used for cooking. The meat and vegetables had been boiled together in these kettles, and the rations were served in crude portions. The procedure was chaotic, and mismanagement was evident everywhere. Often the meat reached the kitchen too late to be cooked and was kept overnight in the rat- and vermin-infested place. When the supplies arrived in the kitchen, they were tied in nets, marked haphazardly and thrown into the copper kettles, where they cooked a half-hour, four hours, or whatever time pleased the cooks.

No attention was given to the type of meat given to the sick or wounded. A piece of bone, a chunk of fat or gristle— with this a suffering soldier had to be satisfied. Florence attempted to have the meat boned so that it might be palatable and nourishing, but she was informed that to do this would require a New Regulation of the Service. Time and energy were too valuable to fight such "red tape," so the courageous nurse went ahead in her own way to improve conditions.

Three hours were required to serve the four miles of patients, and frequently the food brought to the bedsides was as cold as though it had been kept in an Eskimo igloo for twenty-four hours.

"We have not seen a drop of milk," said one of the nurses in writing home, "and the bread is extremely sour. The butter is most filthy, and the meat is more like moist leather than food. Potatoes we are waiting for until they arrive from France."

Said another nurse, "Eleven men died in the night simply from exhaustion, which, humanly speaking, might have been stopped could I have laid my hand on such nourishment as I knew they ought to have had."

Soon Florence with usual ingenuity had set up a diet or nurses' kitchen, from which on short notice chicken and beef broth, arrowroot, jelly and other appealing delicacies were brought to the patients. She had purchased most of these supplies with her own funds in France, and as soon as word of the desperate need reached England, contributions of supplies and money began to pour in for this purpose.

"Tommy, my boy," said a wounded soldier who had been given arrowroot the morning he had arrived at the hospital, "that's all you'll get into your inside this day and think yourself lucky you have got that. But two hours later if another of them blessed angles did not come entreating me to have just a little chicken broth. Well, I took that, thinking maybe is was early dinner, and before I was done wondering what would happen next, round the nurse came again with a bit o' jelly, and all day long at intervals, they kept on bringing me what they called 'a little nourishment.'

"In the evening, Miss Nightingale, she came and had a look at me and says she, 'I hope you are feeling better.' I could have said, 'Ma'am, I feel as fit as a fighting cock,' but I managed to get out something a bit more polite."

Florence's next problem was that of the hospital laundry. Mismanagement and inefficiency characterized this phase of the work also. At the time of her arrival only six shirts were being washed a month for the thousand or more wounded. One reason for this was the fact that if the men sent their shirts to be laundered they were liable to be stolen. Consequently, unless they could persuade the wives of soldiers living near to do their laundry they preferred to wear their soiled garments and hope that they would be washed in the not too distant future.

Florence discovered that the clothing and bed linen of those suffering from infectious diseases was not separated from that used by the wounded, and she found, furthermore, that the bed linen was being merely doused in cold water, which, of course, did not kill the vermin.

Using her own money and contributions she rented a near-by house in which she had boilers installed, hired soldiers' wives, and within a week a hospital laundry was in operation.

When their ship was within sight of the shore, one of the nurses had raced to Florence and said, "Oh, Miss Nightingale, when we land, don't let there be any red tape delays. Let us get straight to nursing the poor fellows." To which she cryptically replied, "The strongest will be wanted at the wash tub." And to the tubs they had gone.

A vexing problem was that of knowing how to provide clothing and linens for the patients while theirs was being washed. The solution demanded that she furnish with her own funds, meager though they were, ten thousand shirts for the men. One reason for the deplorable lack of clothing was the fact that the men had disembarked in the Crimea without their knapsacks, for it was expected that within a few days Sebastopol would fall. Consequently, when the soldiers were wounded, they were destitute of clothing except for that which they were wearing. This was ragged beyond description, dirty beyond degree, blood-soaked, vermin-infested. In fact, Florence saw that this clothing was fit only to be burned.

While the tireless nurse was laboring to improve the laundry facilities and organize the management of the kitchen, she constantly tramped the wards and performed routine duty. Either of these tasks was more than the average person could carry, but Florence found time and energy for any duty. She said, writing to the War Minister, "Nursing is the least important of the functions into which I have been forced."

Whatever Florence's conception of nursing, to the sick and wounded it was a blessing from heaven. Frequently she spent hours on her knees dressing wounds and comforting the dying men. She was known to work for twenty hours without stopping for a rest, directing the placing of the wounded, distributing supplies, supervising the nurses, assisting with operations. Often her presence and encouragement gave a patient new courage.

A surgeon, whom she assisted with major operations, noted her pallor and the tight-shut lips which showed what she was enduring. He also saw the wounded boys' eyes meet hers, and he remembered the gracious answering glance, the gentle assuring voice.

Said the physician, "I believe there was never a severe case of any kind that escaped her notice. The severe cases were the care of her work."

On one occasion she saw five men whose condition the doctor had described as hopeless, but Florence, assisted by a nurse, tended them all night, fed them with a spoon, washed their wounds and eased their sufferings. In the morning they were able to undergo the necessary surgical treatment. At another time she found a soldier about to have his arm amputated, but believing that the limb could be saved, she asked that the operation be delayed. Patiently she nursed the lad, and at length won her case, thus saving a mangled soldier from going through life with one arm.

When cholera or plague cases arrived, she worked untiringly with the patients, even during the final stages of the disease. The more severe the case, the more certain that she would be found bending over the suffering soldier ministering to him in whatever manner would bring comfort. Never did she relax her attention until death or health claimed the patient.

The men idolized her, and as her shadow passed through the corridors and fell upon their beds, they kissed it reverently. As she went from row to row of beds—four miles of them—the men saluted her as though she were the Queen.

Said one soldier, expressing the feelings of all, "If the Queen came for to die, they ought to make her Queen."

"If the soldiers were told that the roof had opened and she had gone visibly to heaven," said a member of Parliament who visited Scutari, "they would not be the least surprised."

Close to the midnight hour, when all was still, quietly, with a lamp in her hand, Florence made a final tour of the wards. She loved them all—those men whom God and England had entrusted to her care.

"It seemed an endless walk," a friend reported who accompanied her. ". . . As we slowly passed along, the silence was profound; very seldom did a moan or cry from these deeply suffering ones fall on our ears. A dim light burned here and there. Miss Nightingale carried her lantern which she set down before she bent over any of the patients. I much admired her manner to the men, it was so tender and kind."

Longfellow immortalized this nightly tour in his well-known poem, in which he speaks of Florence as "the lady with the lamp."

> Lo! In that hour of misery,
> A lady with a lamp I see
> Pass through the glimmering gloom,
> And flit from room to room.
> And slow, as in a dream of bliss,
> The speechless sufferer turns to kiss
> Her shadow as it falls
> Upon the darkening walls.

By Christmas day, 1854, less than two months after she and the band of nurses landed at Scutari, where there had been filth, hunger and loneliness there was cleanliness, wholesome food and the reassuring presence of someone who "cared." Florence Nightingale brought the comfort of a sympathetic hand and heart, and a light that glowed in the shadow of death.

When engaging the soldiers' wives to do the hospital laundry, Florence discovered the terrible plight of these women. Some wives had been granted permission to accompany their husbands on foreign service, and if for any reason they became separated, there was no one to care for them. Many wives and sweethearts followed the army, and of course, neither food nor lodging was provided. These women, the majority of whom were respectable, Florence discovered were living in holes and corners of the Barrack Hospital.

Their clothes were rags, and they had neither shoes nor covering for their heads. Some had found quarters in the dark basement rooms. Living more like rats than humans, they ate their scanty meals, nursed their sick and brought their babies into the world.

Florence's soul was stirred by the sad plight of these women, and she sent them food from her private supply. Mrs. Bracebridge began the work of bettering their condition, and eventually a house was obtained. The women cleaned this home and Florence, using private funds, furnished it. A ward for their sick was opened in the upper part of the laundry. Work was secured for many of the women in Constantinople and a school was started for the children.

When Lady Alicia Blackwood, who had come with her husband to Scutari, asked what she could do, Florence replied, "In this barrack are now located some two hundred poor women in the most abject misery . . . They are in rags and covered with vermin. My heart bleeds for them; but my work is with the soldiers, not with their wives. Now, will you undertake to look after them?"

At once Lady Blackwood undertook the work, and no detail was overlooked.

Florence found much in the hospital to challenge her prowess. She observed that many operations were performed in the wards, and she arranged that screens be used so that other patients would not be tortured by seeing the misery of their comrades.

"When a poor fellow," she said, "who is to be amputated tomorrow sees his comrade today die under the knife it makes impressions and diminishes his chances. The mortality of the operations is frightful."

Since at that time the use of anaesthetics was virtually unknown, the suffering was terrific. The head medical officer advised against the use of chloroform, and declared that "the smart of the knife is a powerful stimulant, and it is better to hear a man bawl lustily than to see him sink silently into the grave."

Florence decided to provide stationary and postage for the men in the wards, and urged them, if they were able, to write home and thus relieve their tension. Florence wrote many letters to the men's families and she also asked the nurses to write letters dictated by the men who were unable to write their own messages. When a soldier died, Florence wrote letters to the family in which she sent details of his death.

Her active mind never wearied of planning for the soldiers' betterment. She established a money-order department through which soldiers could send their pay home. As a result, many thousands of pounds eventually went to their families which otherwise would have been wasted. Roused to action by the evil of saloons and other places where liquor was sold, she started a coffee house to offset this. She became the leader of a movement which finds its modern counterpart in the USO, and established reading rooms, recreational activities and classrooms for the men.

Nor did she forget the nurses' families which had been left behind but constantly wrote letters to friends urging concern for their welfare. Florence's mother said, "Flo has been writing incessantly lately about the nurses' families, for whom the best seem getting very anxious. And she scarcely mentions anything else."

Her correspondence was heavy, and she once said, "I nurse all day and write all night." Another arduous task was dispensing the supplies and gratuities which she provided or which was contributed for special purposes by friends.

"I am a kind of general dealer," she wrote the War Minister, "in socks, shirts, knives and forks, wooden spoons, tin baths, tables and forms, cabbages and carrots, operating tables, towels and soap, small pillows, small toothcombs, precipitate for destroying lice, bedpans, stump pillows. I will send you a picture of my caravanserai into which beasts come in and out, the 'beasts' being the vermin."

Sidney Osborne, a minister present at the time, described the quarters, which he called the Sisters' Tower, where Florence and her staff lived:

"Entering the door you at once see a busy and interesting scene. There is a large room with two or three doors on one side, and on the other, one door opening into an apartment where many of the nurses sleep. The floor on one side of the large room was loaded with stores of things, bales of shirts, socks, slippers, dressing gowns, flannel . . .

" 'From this room,' wrote a volunteer, 'were distributed arrowroot, sago, rice puddings, jelly, beef tea, lemonade.' Orderlies were waiting at the door with requisitions. We used to call this the Tower of Babel. In the middle of the day everything and everybody seemed to be there; boxes, parcels, bundles of sheets, shirts and old linen, sugar, bread, kettles, saucepans, heaps of books, ladies, nuns, nurses, orderlies, Turks, Greeks, French and Italian servants, officers, waiting to see Miss Nightingale . . . all speaking their own language."

Often, despite the desperate activity and the horrible suffering, there were humorous situations. A nurse one day announced to Florence, "I came out, ma'am, prepared to submit to everything, to be put upon in every way. But there are some things one can't submit to. There is the caps, ma'am, that suits one face, and some that suits another. And if I'd known, ma'am, about the caps, great as was my desire to come out to nurse at Scutari, I wouldn't have come, ma'am." With her usual efficiency Florence sought to solve this girl's difficulty with the seriousness with which she undertook to alleviate the sufferings of the wounded.

All her time was not spent in performing these seemingly endless duties. Florence also shouldered the heavier task of reforming and reorganizing the system which had produced the chaotic conditions. She found in the overlapping of agencies and departments a constant source of friction. In many cases the following officers or groups must take action before a needed reform could be instituted: the Secretary of State, the War Office and the Secretary of War, the House Guards, the Ordinance Department, the Victualling Office, the Transport Office, the Army Medical Department and the Treasury.

For example, if Florence found it necessary to have unused and dilapidated wards or buildings repaired quickly to care for the hundreds of wounded who were arriving constantly, the expenditure must first be authorized by the London Medical Board. This authorization was then submitted to the House Guards, then to the Ordnance Department and finally to the Treasury. These departments must act favorably upon the request, a process which required weeks before the work could be started.

At last in desperation she decided to take the matter into her own hands and became a liason officer between these departments. She engaged and paid workmen, and while the boards were transferring the orders from rank to rank and from lower to superior officers, she had the work done and accommodations were ready when the sufferers arrived.

On one occasion when shirts were urgently needed, resourceful Florence found 27,000 in a storeroom where they had been unloaded, but she could not unpack them until a board "sat" and ordered disposal of the garments. Calling the board for action, she discovered that many of the members were away. Consequently, for three weeks no shirts could be obtained, except for those which Florence furnished with her own funds. This was not the only example of uncoordinated authority; such instances were daily occurrences. She exposed evidence of jealous department heads and a struggle to gain authority.

Of all the departments, that which supervised the orderlies was most chaotic. These men were usually convalescents from the army ranks and they were returned to active service as soon as possible. Consequently, though they did their work well, they took no interest in acquiring more knowledge or becoming more efficient either in assigned duties or activities related to their work.

Often it was their task to secure and dispense supplies, but they never knew where to find them. On one occasion when chloride of lime was needed, three times the request received this reply: "There is none." Florence insisted that a thorough search be made, and eventually she discovered ninety pounds in a place where any orderly should have been able to find it.

"If the convalescents," she suggested in her report of corrective and remedial measures with respect to the orderlies, "being good orderlies, were not sent away to the Crimea as soon as they have learnt their work, if the commander-in-chief would call upon the commanding officer of each regiment to select ten men from each as hospital orderlies or from a depot here, not young soldiers, but men of good character, this would give some hope of organizing an efficient corps. The orderlies ought to be well paid, well fed, well housed. They are now overworked, ill fed, ill housed."

The problem of shipping supplies from England distressed Florence. Troubled by the mismanagement, she determined to initiate corrective measures. For example, hospital beds arrived, but their legs had been sent to the Crimea. Needed medical stores were often packed under stacks of ammunition, and could be unpacked only after this cargo, unneeded at the time, had been unloaded. On one occasion a supply of boots arrived—all of which would fit only the left foot!

"There are no storehouses," Florence wrote the home office authorities, "by the water's edge, and portage is expensive and slow." She suggested that a government warehouse be established to solve this difficulty.

Neither at Scutari nor Constantinople was there an office for reception or delivery of supplies. Hence, if goods arrived for the hospital in merchant vessels, the supplies were needlessly detained in the Turkish Custom House, and the task of releasing them entailed exasperating delay, confusion and difficulty. Eventually many of the provisions were lost, destroyed or damaged, and Florence wrote of this situation, "The Custom House is a bottomless pit, whence nothing ever issued of all that was thrown in."

While planning a supervisory organization, she discovered the fact that various supplies, regardless of their nature or destination were landed and stored together. Frequently ships made three trips between Balaclava and Scutari with desperately needed supplies before they were landed at Scutari.

She wrote Sidney Herbert, War Minister, about the urgency of having these supplies unloaded promptly and where needed:

"English people look upon Scutari as a place of inns and hackney coaches and houses to let furnished. It required yesterday to land twenty-five casks of sugar, four oxen and two men six hours . . . There are no pack horses and no asses, except those used by the peasantry . . . Four days in the week we cannot communicate with Constantinople except by the other harbor, one and a quarter miles off, to which the road is almost impassable."

A primary cause for the condition in which the wounded arrived at Scutari was the lack of proper clothing. "The state of the troops who return here," Florence wrote, "is frostbitten, seminude, ragged." A nurse said, in writing of this problem, "The men who came from the Front had on only thin linen shirts to keep out the severe Crimean frost. When they were carried in on the stretchers, their clothing had to be cut away. In most cases the flesh and clothes were frozen together; and as for the feet, the boots had to be cut off bit by bit, the flesh coming off with them. In the mornings the sinews and bones were laid bare."

Florence demanded clothing for the soldiers. "If the troops are not supplied with warm clothing, Napoleon's Russian campaign will be repeated here," she warned.

In every feature of the work, her own as well as that of related departments and officers, she had a keen eye for detail and was tirelessly seeking methods of accomplishing needed reforms. Within a few months of her arrival she sent through the proper channels a long report in which she stated the existing evils of mismanagement and suggested remedial steps to be taken promptly. She could not leave unsolved a problem caused by lack of organization or a proper authority, and, she was quick to demand proper action.

Busy day and night in the wards, assisting at the operating tables, she grasped the staggering problems of organization and supply, and she bombarded the authorities in England with letters demanding action and presenting plans for needed changes.

Often Sir Sidney Herbert, the Secretary of War and Florence's close friend, received a chain of letters from the gallant nurse. She did not present her suggestions merely to the chief of staff, but appealed to any officer who might help to bring order out of the Scutari chaos. Chiding, bamboozling, threatening, she demanded that proper remedial orders be taken without snail-paced delay.

Her only aim was to bring needed relief to those wounded sons of England to whom she was ministering in the Name of the Master. As a result of her persistent reports and letters, a Sanitary Commission was appointed early in 1855 to investigate her charges, and when this group found that conditions were as she described them, it set in motion the machinery which would better them.

Chapter 7

THE POPULAR HEROINE

FLORENCE HAD WON her way into the wounded soldiers' hearts. Once left to rot in rags, they were now cared for by skilled and sympathetic hands. The work of the nurses was successful and received glowing tributes everywhere. Florence resented the slightest suggestion which would in any way affect the women under her leadership.

Sir Herbert, however, decided that she needed assistance and dispatched without Florence's knowledge forty-six additional nurses. Their arrival brought consternation to the leader's soul, for she felt that the War Minister had overstepped the bounds of authority and imposed his will upon hers. Consequently she wrote him this message:

"You have sacrificed the cause so dear to my heart. You have sacrificed your own written word to a popular cry. You must feel that I ought to resign, where conditions are imposed on me which render the object for which I am employed unattainable, and I only remain at my post till I have provided in some measure for these poor wanderers . . .

"Had I the enormous folly at the end of eleven days' experience to require more women, would it not seem that you, as a statesman, should have said, 'Wait till you can see your way better'? But I made no such request."

Florence was justified in her resentment, for the nurses had not only been sent without her permission or advice but had been directed to report to other officials rather than to her. This action undermined her authority, and she knew that all power in her realm should be centered in one person. This opened the way for similar action, which destroyed the system she had laboriously established.

The arrival of the additional nurses presented, moreover, many practical difficulties, of which Bracebridge wrote, "The forty-six have fallen on us like a cloud of locusts. Where to house them, feed them, place them, is difficult; how to care for them not to be imagined."

Florence was not one to permit a slight to interfere with the efficient execution of her duties as a nurse. The wounded men were of primary importance, and she threw all her energy into making readjustments made necessary by the change in policy. Some of the nurses were sent to other hospitals and even to Balaclava. Eventually, however, they were all fitted into the hospital pattern as the war progressed, and more were requested. At the close of the conflict Florence had a hundred and twenty-five efficient and well-trained nurses under her care.

The Scutari work was now progressing favorably, and the rate of mortality had declined sharply. As spring came the number of patients decreased. But Florence knew that the wounded would increase when the siege of Sebastopol became an active campaign with assaults and direct charges, and she was eager to inspect the hospitals provided for the soldiers at Balaclava as the wounded were taken there if possible so that the agonizing sea trip to Scutari might be avoided.

In the Crimea there were four general hospitals in addition to the regimental hospitals she wished to visit, which were the General Hospital at Balaclava, the Castle Hospital, consisting of huts on Genoese Heights above the General Hospital, the St. George's Monastery Hospital and that of the Land Transport Corps. On May 2, 1855, Florence set out for the Crimea and a general visit to the various units organized to care for the wounded.

"Steaming up the Bosphorus and across the Black Sea," she wrote May 5, " with four nurses, two cooks, a boy, to Crim Tartary, to overhaul the Regimental Hospitals, in the *Robert Lowe* or the *Robert Slow*, for an exceedingly slow boat it is, taking back 420 of her patients, a draught of convalescents returning to their regiments to be shot again."

Florence's first visit was to Lord Raglan, Commander of the Forces. She made the trip on horseback, and her cavalcade attracted much attention as it wound its way through the roads crowded with mules, artillery, cannon, foot soldiers, destroyed vehicles and frightened and rearing mounts. But Florence was grateful for this privilege of seeing the men active in their war duties.

"Fancy working five nights out of seven in the trenches," she wrote a few days later in a letter which was ultimately forwarded to Windsor Castle. "Fancy being thirty-six hours in them at a stretch, or half lying down, often forty-eight hours with no food but raw salt pork, sprinkled with sugar, rum and biscuit; nothing hot, because the exhausted soldier could not collect his own fuel, as he was expected to do, to cook his own ration. And fancy, through all this, the army preserving their courage and patience, as they have done, and being now eager, the old ones more than the young ones, to be led even into the trenches. There was something sublime in the spectacle."

After the visit to the trenches and the ceremonial visit to the commander, the valiant nurse began an inspection tour of the hospitals. For many days she continued the tour, suggesting the building of new huts, planning special diet kitchens, seeing if the nurses performed their duties efficiently. Here as at her Scutari base she was unafraid of contagious diseases and nursing soldiers who had been fever-stricken.

One evening, on returning to her quarters, she complained of unusual weariness, and in the morning discovered that she was the prey of Crimean fever. The soldiers viewed this as a misfortune, but it was a God-directed providence, for Florence's work in directing the women's nursing corps could be continued by others, whereas there remained for her a greater task to be achieved in the homeland. At once she was taken to the Castle Hospital on the Genoese Heights, where she was described as "very near death."

The rapidly spreading news of Florence's illness was the cause of great concern in official governmental and army circles. The Nightingales, now justly proud of their famous Flo, prayed earnestly that God's healing hand would be laid upon their daughter.

"The soldiers turned their faces to the wall and cried," said an observer, for their dearest friend was in evident danger. There was not one who would not have gladly taken her place and given his life for her. In time the crisis passed, and Lord Raglan telegraphed the news to England, where the bulletins were forwarded to the Queen, who wrote, "Truly thankful to learn that excellent and valuable person, Miss Nightingale, is safe."

While Florence was convalescing the attending doctors advised her to recuperate in England, which she refused to do, convinced that she was a front-trench worker and not a homeland lassie. Reviewing her work, she saw that it was well organized and functioned efficiently. She had laid the ground-work well but decided that she could not yet be spared. Shortly she demanded to return to Scutari, where she was royally welcomed. Officials were at the pier to meet her, and as she was borne on a stretcher from the vessel the soldiers vied with each other in helping to carry the precious burden.

"I do not remember anything during the campaign," said a member of Florence's homecoming party, "so gratifying to the feelings as that simple though grand procession."

Her recovery was slow, and later she moved from Scutari to Therapia, in an effort to regain her strength. She was so weak at times that she could hardly speak above a whisper, and her family and friends, especially Sir Sidney Herbert, begged—and almost demanded—that she return to England. But Florence adamantly refused, for she believed that here in the midst of her triumph scenes she would eventually regain strength to shoulder her burdens. Their reaction to her illness and recovery showed how deeply the English people, as well as the people of the world, appreciated her fine spirit, her loyalty to a cause dear to her heart, and the inspiring example she gave to the world of a sacrificial personality.

"The feeling in every soul," wrote her sister to a friend, "so wide and deep, touches us more than I can tell. Heavy, red-faced old fox-hunting squires who never had a sentiment in their lives come with their eyes full of tears; narrow-minded farmers with both eyes on the main chance are melted; young ladies who never got beyond their balls and concerts are warmed.

"The bookseller says that a general or admiral can be replaced, but that there can be no successor to Miss Nightingale. A ship owner wants to call a new vessel after her. Lady Dunsany says Joan of Arc was not more a creation of the moment and for the moment than Florence. Lady Byron says that even her illness will advance her work, as all things must for those who do all with His aid."

Daily her fame leaped all fences and raced to humble homes, to castles and even to the Queen's abode. Lavish expressions of appreciation came from every place and all types of persons. Florence Nightingale became the heroine of the cottage, the workshop, the alley and the boulevards. Printers rushed through their presses pamphlets containing woodcuts and verses praising "The Lady with the Lamp." One verse became so popular that it lingered for many years:

> So forward, my lads, may your hearts never fail,
> You are cheered by the presence of a sweet Nightingale.

Newspapers—the nation's most influential—and magazines —even the smallest country journals—overflowed with verse celebrating her fame. Prizes were given for poems written about her. Songs with sentimental titles became popular: "The Woman's Smile," "The Shadow on the Pillow," "The Star of the East" and dozens of others. Her picture appeared on writing paper, and her name was used in connection with a variety of animate and inanimate objects. Even race horses were named after her. Tradesmen printed on their paper bags portraits and short biographical sketches of the famous nurse. Constantly the people sought new methods of showing their regard for her.

Parthe expressed the sentiment of the English, commoners and titled alike, when she said, "The people love you with a sort of passionate tenderness that goes to my heart."

"I do not affect indifference to real sympathy," Florence wrote to her sister, "but I have felt painfully the éclat that has been given to this adventure. The small, still beginning, the simple hardship, the silent and gradual struggle upward, these are the climate in which an enterprise really thrives and grows. Time has not altered our Saviour's lesson on that point."

Expressions of love and admiration assumed a more permanent form than verse, songs, portraits, paper bags and racehorses. When the homeland received news of her recovery and determination to remain at the front until the war was won, a movement was forthwith started to commemorate in a public manner her devotion and services. Some favored a personal gift, but Lady Herbert, knowing that this would displease "the Lady with the Lamp," wrote to Florence for her opinion regarding the nature of this monument.

In reply to the request Florence, with characteristic bluntness, said, "People seem to think I have nothing to do but sit here and form plans. If the public choose to recognize my services and my judgment in this matter, they must leave those services and that judgment unfettered."

Someone suggested that an institution be established similar to the Kaiserwerth organization, but Florence refused to suggest a plan. The idea, however, had taken root too deeply in popular fancy to be torn out easily and a committee of influential people, including Sir Herbert, the War Minister, was formed. This group decided to raise a fund to establish a school for nurses under a council appointed by Florence. A public meeting was announced for November 29, 1855, to give expression to the general feeling that her services in the war-zone hospitals be given grateful recognition by the British commonwealth. The Duke of Cambridge presided, showing thus the blessing of the royal family.

"The most interesting day of thy mother's life," wrote Mrs. Nightingale to her daughter in the Crimea. "You will be more indifferent than any of us to your fame, but be glad that we feel this is a proud day for us. The Duke of Cambridge was in the chair and made a simple, manly speech. Sidney Herbert delighted everyone. Lord Stanley, the Duke of Argyle and Sir J. Pakington spoke capitally. Moncton Milnes was very touching, Lord Lansdowne as good as in his best days."

The War Minister read sections from the soldiers' letters

wherein they expressed their feelings regarding her work and what it had meant to their disconsolate lives. Moncton Milnes drew a vivid contrast between the brilliant scene before him and that "noble woman devoting herself to the service of her suffering fellow creatures on the black shores of the Crim Tartary, overlooking the waters of the inhospitable sea."

These praises meant little, if anything, to Florence, whose highest desire was to serve her Master diligently and seek such recognition as would advance the cause she represented. Her feelings, however, were expressed in a letter to her parents:

"If my name and my having done what I could for God and mankind have given you pleasure, that is a real pleasure to me. My reputation has not been a boon to me in my work; but if you have been pleased that is enough. I shall live my name now and shall feel that it is the greatest return that you can find satisfaction in hearing your child named, and in feeling that her work draws sympathies together. Life is sweet after all."

As a result of the meeting, a Nightingale Fund was established to enable her to found and control an institute for the training, sustenance and protection of paid and unpaid nurses. In acknowledgement of this signal honor, she wrote this letter to Sir Sidney:

"In answer to your letter proposing to me the undertaking of a Training School for Nurses, I will first beg to say that it is impossible for me to express what I have felt in regard to the sympathy and the confidence shown to me by the originators and supporters of this scheme. Exposed as I am to be misinterpreted and misunderstood, in a field of action in which the work is new, complicated and distant from many who sit in judgment upon it, it is indeed an abiding support to have such sympathy and such appreciation brought home to me in the midst of labor and difficulties all but over-powering.

"I must add, however, that my present work is such as I would never desert for any other, so long as I see room to believe that what I may do here is unfinished. May I then beg you to express to the Committee that I accept their proposal, provided that I may do so on their understanding of this great uncertainty as to when it will be possible for me to carry it out."

Public meetings in support of the Fund were held throughout the British Empire, and contributions flowed in. The front-line soldiers sent liberal gifts. Jenny Lind, the world-famous Swedish singer, gave a concert the proceeds of which were approximately ten thousand dollars. Lord Stanley, in a speech given at one of the meetings, summarized graphically the work which Florence had accomplished.

"There is no part of England," he said, "no city or county, scarcely a considerable village, where some cottage household has not been comforted amidst its mourning for the loss of one who had fallen in the war by the assurance that his last moments were watched and his worst sufferings soothed by that care, at once tender and skillful, which no man and few women could have shown.

"True heroism is not so plentiful that we can afford to let it pass unrecognized . . . And with the exception of Howard, the prison reformer, I know no person besides Miss Nightingale within the last one hundred years within this island, or perhaps in Europe, who has voluntarily encountered dangers so imminent and undertaken offices so repulsive, working for a large and worthy object in a pure spirit of duty toward God and compassion for man."

Queen Victoria, desiring to show personal gratitude for her brave deeds, wrote Florence shortly after the public meeting and sent her a jeweled decoration.

"You are, I know," said the letter, "well aware of the high sense I entertain of the Christian devotion which you have displayed during this great and bloody war, and I need hardly repeat to you how warm my admiration is for your services which are fully equal to those of my dear and brave soldiers whose sufferings you have had the privilege of alleviating in so merciful a manner which I trust will be agreeable to you, and therefore send you with this letter a brooch, the form and emblem of which commemorate your great and blessed work, and which I hope you will wear as a mark of the highest appreciation of your Sovereign.

"It will be a very great satisfaction to me, when you return to these shores, to make the acquaintance of one who has set so bright an example to our sex."

The jewel, designed by the Prince Consort, resembled a badge rather than a brooch, and bore the St. George's Cross and the royal cipher, surmounted by a crown of diamonds. The inscription "Blessed Are the Merciful" encircled the badge on which appeared also the word "Crimea." On the reverse was the inscription "To Miss Florence Nightingale, as a mark of esteem and gratitude for her devotion toward the Queen's brave soldiers. From Victoria R., 1855."

While all these tokens of appreciation and honor were being showered upon her, Florence was going ahead unremittingly with her work. Sebastopol fell on September 8, 1855. Hospitals were filled to overflowing and there were many new graves. On October 8, Florence left Scutari for Balaclava, and the following month rushed back to her former base where a cholera epidemic had laid siege to the soldiers. On March 21, 1856, she returned once more to Balaclava, where conditions urgently demanded her supervision, and here she remained until the war was over.

During these tragedy-packed months she performed her hardest work of the war. Because the Crimean hospitals were some distance from each other, Florence frequently spent entire days riding horseback through the cold and over the almost impassable roads from hospital to hospital. Sometimes the trips were made in a jostling cart drawn over the rough roads by an often cranky army mule whose disposition had been ruined months before by the fiery temper of a belligerent top sergeant. When the roads were impassible either by horse or mule cart, Florence set out on foot. Nothing could daunt or deter her in this purpose of serving the wounded.

"To return from those places [the hospitals] at night," said one who accompanied her, "was a very dangerous experience, as the road led across a very uneven country. It was still more perilous when snow was on the ground. I have seen her stand for hours at the top of a bleak rocky mountain near the hospital giving her instructions while the snow was falling heavily."

She superintended the nursing in all the hospitals under her charge, established reading rooms, improved the water supply near the hospitals, covered the huts with felt for protection against the winter cold and established sufficient additional diet kitchens to care for the growing needs.

"We cooked all the extra diets for five hundred to six hundred patients," she wrote to the War Minister's wife "and the whole diet for the wounded officers by ourselves in a shed. I could not get an extra diet kitchen built, promised me in May, till I came up this time to do it myself in October. During the whole of this time, every egg, every bit of butter, jelly, ale and eau de cologne which the sick officers have had was provided out of Mrs. Samuel Smith's or my private pocket. On November 4, I opened my extra diet kitchen."

Although at Scutari she had fought through a tangle of opposition and misunderstanding from those higher in official authority, she found this antagonism more intense in the Crimea, which added to the burden of her work. Here she met with jealousy, indifference and contemptuous remarks that "her ideas were fads."

"There is not an official," she said to a friend, "who would not burn me like Joan of Arc, if he could." A rather sweeping statement this in view of the fact that many of her staunch friends were among the highest officers! But Florence had so exposed the inefficiency, mismanagement and obstinacy of the officials responsible for the Crimean debacle among the wounded that they smarted under her scathing criticism which at times nearly cost them their positions.

Said Florence to Sir Herbert, "Dr. Hall is attempting to root me out of the Crimea." The doctor in question was the principal medical officer in the Crimean sector and partially responsible for the appalling health conditions she had fearlessly exposed. He did not admire her, nor was he willing to admit the value of her work. She found the food supply and distributing branch of the service to be critically deficient and she declared the fact boldly.

"We have now been ten days without rations," she wrote on March 24, 1856, six days before the war ended. "Lord Cardigan was surprised to find his horses die at the end of a fortnight because they were without rations, and said that they 'chose to do it, obstinate brutes.' The Inspector-General and Purveyors wish to see whether women can live as long as horses without rations. I thank God my charge has felt neither cold nor hunger and is in efficient order, having cooked and administered in both hospitals the whole of the extras for 260 beds, ever since the first day of their arrival . . .

"I have however felt both . . . For during these ten days I have fed and warmed those women at my own private expense by my own private exertions. I have never been off my horse till nine or ten at night, except when it was too dark to walk home over these crags, even with a lantern, when I have gone on foot. During the greater part of the day, I have been without food necessarily, except a little . . . water. But the object of my coming has been attained, and my women have neither starved nor suffered."

Despite opposition and hardship, the work of tenderly caring for the sick went on. Florence's energy was so exhausted by exposure and hardship caused by lack of co-operation among army officials that a few weeks before the war ended she made arrangements for her own funeral, fearing that death was near. Her final thought, however, was for the army, and after naming various requests, she said:

"I would wish that I could have done something more to prove to the noble army whom I have so cared for, my respect and esteem. If the commander-of-forces would put into General Orders a message of farewell from me, of remembrance of the time when we lived and suffered and worked together, I should be grateful to him."

However, it was not God's will that Florence should die. There were yet other fields into which she must enter. Though unappreciated by many with whom she had lived and whom she had efficiently served, yet her work was to be a great blessing in years to come. Her achievements in the field of nursing did more to offset the damages and ravages which came with the discovery of gunpowder than any other force or combination of personalities. On ambulance ships, hospital airplanes, in jungle hospitals erected under coconut groves, thousands of nurses have streamed from the fountain of service which she opened.

The war came to a close March 30, 1856, but since there was much to be done in the hospitals, Florence remained until July, when a British man-of-war was offered for her trip home. The country was ready to receive her with open arms. Receptions were planned and triumphal arches were to be erected. Mayors prepared speeches. Some suggested that her carriage be drawn by the nation's élite and that bands welcome her train. In fact, the nation teemed with plans by which it sought to honor and show esteem for this noble woman who served the Master and the people.

Florence's plans, however, did not coincide with the wishes of the people who sought to honor her. Using an assumed name, the humble, Christlike nurse took a small steamer, stayed one night in Paris at an insignificant hotel, spent a few hours in a London convent, entrained for Lea Hurst as an unknown passenger, walked wearily from the railroad station and entered her home by the rear door on August 7, 1856, having done in the Master's Name a work whose blessings are today enjoyed around the world.

Chapter 8

THE PRACTICAL REFORMER

RETURNING INCOGNITO TO ENGLAND did not achieve Florence's desire, to attain privacy and avoid publicity. Her work in Scutari had thrust her into the national limelight and the nation wanted not only to hear but to see her. This was the desire of those in the humblest hut and the imperial palace. So unselfish and effective was her sacrifice for others that her fellow countrymen demanded to know the details of her work to correct the blunders which before Florence's arrival had endangered the health of the soldiers fighting the Crimean War.

Her labors at Scutari were, as she expressed it, "child's play" in comparison with what was accomplished later. Her body pleaded for rest and recuperation; her mental tension clamored for release; her physical endurance required replenishment. However, so urgent were the changes which must be made in army medical practice that she could not remain at home. She had seen the vision and was willing to make any sacrifice demanded to achieve the goal.

Florence craved a nursing career and sought to establish nursing as a profession, an aim encouraged by the people's generous interest in establishing a training school for nurses.

But Florence knew that first she must unburden her soul, and with the zeal of a reformer she threw all her energies into reorganizing the military medical program.

"No one can feel for the army as I do," she said in a note to a friend. "These people who talk to us have all fed their children on the fat of the land and dressed them in velvet and silk, while we have been away. I have had to see my children dressed"—she referred to the wounded soldiers as her "children"—"in a dirty blanket and an old pair of regimental trousers, and to see them fed on raw salt meat; and nine thousand of my children are lying, from cases which might have been prevented, in their forgotten graves. But I can never forget. People must have seen that long dreadful winter to know what it was."

She unearthed facts to sustain her contention that of the forty-six hundred soldiers who died, most of them would have recovered had suitable equipment and care been available. She showed that among troops the mortality rate from disease alone was 60 per cent, whereas improved sanitation, food and nursing in the hospitals reduced the death rate sharply.

During the first few weeks following her return, she received letters, gifts, requests for addresses and a thousand other communications. "Hailstorms of letters"—thus her sister described the mass of missives that flocked to her like homing pigeons. On August 23, 1856, came an important message signed by Sir James Clark, physician to Queen Victoria, wherein he invited the nurse to his home at Birk Hall. He wrote that not only would the Scottish air be beneficial to her health but that the court would soon take up residence at Balmoral and the Queen would invite Florence to visit her. The Queen approved of the present invitation and would no doubt find opportunity at Birk Hall for quiet and informal talks in addition to the command visit to Balmoral.

Florence flung her challenge to the nation—a spirited challenge.

"You cannot do more for those who have suffered and died in their country's service," she said. "They need our help no longer. Their spirits are with God who gave them. It remains for us to strive that their sufferings may not have been endured in vain, to endeavor so to learn from experience as to lessen such sufferings in the future by forethought and wise management."

Forgetting her body's demand for rest, Florence flung herself into the battle to achieve this one goal.

"I stand on the altar of the murdered men," she wrote in her private notes in 1856, "and while I live, I fight their cause."

These words had reached the Queen's ear and action was being demanded. She had seen the vision God had given her, and she was not content until it became more tangible than the flimsy stuff of which dreams are made.

Before going to the Queen's Scottish residence, Florence gathered needed statistics to prove her contention that improved medical care of the soldiers would reduce the fatalities among them. The valiant crusader planned a written report in which she would present a summary of her findings and suggest a plan of reform. First there must be a reformation commission and she decided to ask for a Royal Commission to inquire into the complex problem of barracks, hospitals and the Army Medical Department. She was interested especially in the latter for she had suffered intensely as a result of the stiff-headed idiocy of jealous medical officers.

"You cannot improve the sanitary care of an army in the field," she declared, "if the medical service in the field is deficient; if sanitary science is neglected in the hospitals, it is more probable that such defects exist at home."

Following this trail of thought with the persistence of a prowling bloodhound, Florence discovered the appalling fact

that among men between the ages of twenty to thirty-five
the army death rate was double that of the civilian rate, and
this was established by the observation of hand-picked
soldiers.

"This is as criminal," Florence declared, "as it would
be to take a thousand men yearly out on Salisbury Plain
and shoot them."

Such statements aroused army ire, and medical men in
high positions, where they had soft-cushioned themselves in
the Queen's military service, cowered under the barrage.
Her one desire and indomitable determination was that jus-
tice be shown the fighting men, and as she stood beside the
graves at Scutari, some of which she had helped to dig, she
lifted her voice and the Queen heard.

The visit lasted a month, and two days after her arrival
at Birk Hall she met the Queen and Prince Consort at Balmoral, where, as the Prince noted in his diary, "she put
before us all the defects of our present military hospital
system and the reforms that are needed and we are much
pleased with her. She is extremely modest." A few days
later the Queen came to Birk Hall where she had tea with
the nurse to whom God had given the challenge of reform.
"I wish we had her in the War Office," said the Queen after
she and Florence had their "great talk," as Miss Nightingale
described the conference.

The Queen requested her to remain in Scotland for an interview with leading officers and members of the government,
Lord Panmure, particularly. The interviews were satisfactory and everyone whom she consulted was favorable to her
plea for the organization of a reform commission. On returning to London, Florence took up residence at the Burlington Hotel, where she formed what was known as her "cabinet
of reformers" with whom she consulted daily. This group,
called "the Little War Office," drew up a list of acts to be
carried out by the Royal Commission and drafted instruc-

tions to be submitted to Lord Panmure, known as "the Bison."

Finally the organization of the Commission was agreed upon even by the slow-moving Bison and Sir Herbert Sidney, long Florence's friend, and it came into being on November 16, 1856, though the royal warrant which established it was not signed until the following May 5. The delay was exasperating both to Florence and Sir Herbert, for while they were trying earnestly to force action, opponents in the War Office and the Army Medical Department were thwarting their efforts.

During this trying period Florence held in reserve the weapon of public appeal, which she knew would get action from the Bison, whom she declared to be "bullyable." She knew the people were supporting her. At Balmoral it had been decided that she make a report with suggestions for action, which if accomplished would obviate the necessity of revealing the findings publicly.

Writing to Sir Herbert, she declared flatly however, "Three months from this date I publish my experience of the Crimean campaign and my suggestions for improvement unless there has been a fair and tangible pledge for reform."

With assiduity she compiled her findings, entitled *Notes Affecting the Health, Efficiency and Hospital Administration of the British Army*. For six months, though her health was poor and her energy depleted, Florence labored at the arduous task of writing by hand this report, consisting of hundreds of pages, which she printed at her own expense and circulated among friends, where the report gained praise.

"It is a mine of facts and inferences," wrote Sir John McNeill, who, having been sent in 1855 to the East by government orders, was familiar with the subject, "which will furnish materials for every scheme that is likely to be built up for several generations. It contains a body of information and instruction such as no one else . . . has ever brought to bear upon any similar subject. I regard it as a gift to the army and to the country altogether priceless."

Beginning with an introductory chapter in which she presented a history of the health of the British army in previous campaigns, she described the medical status of the soldiers in the recently-ended Crimean War. Then she treated such subjects as the organization of hospitals, regimental and general, the need for sanitary officials in the army, the promotion of a statistical department, the education and advancement of medical officers, soldiers' pay and stoppage, diet and cooking, washing and canteen-establishment, the soldiers' wives, the construction of army hospitals and the comparative mortality of armies in war and peace. She concluded the book with an appendix of supplementary notes, diagrams and illustrations.

The courageous woman pointed out that conditions in army hospitals were only a part of army health. The fact that in the Crimean War seven times the number killed in battle died from disease indicated the poor health of the army in peacetime.

This situation must be changed, Florence said, by total reorganization and the application of sanitary science to the army as a whole.

Her fame spread swiftly as she taxed the abilities of experts in allied strategic fields of military science and the navy asked her to "take up the sailors and to introduce female nurses into the naval hospitals." She was also consulted regarding plans for a naval hospital at Woolwich. "I mean to profit," wrote Sir John Liddell, director general of the navy, "in both our new and old buildings from your clever report on the construction of the hospitals."

"She has sown seed that will give a full harvest," said Sir Robert Rawlinson, "and mankind will be better for her practical labors to the end of time. Hospitals will be constructed according to her wise arrangements, and they will be managed in conformity to her humane rules. One man in the army will be more useful than two formerly, and reason will preside over comfort and health."

Florence made a thorough study of London military and civil hospitals, and she made glowing suggestions for improvements. Reading rooms, started in the Crimea, had proved so successful that the innovation was introduced in England, and she provided funds for such a project at the Aldershot Camp. She wanted to be authentic in the minute details of her report and consulted experts, among them leading architects who furnished her with plans of the best hospitals not only in Great Britain but also on the Continent. She sought dietetic information from the highest authorities and interviewed even army surgeons, missionaries and chaplains.

Florence's "bullying" proved so effective that by April 27, 1857, Lord Panmure called on Florence and presented to her the official draft of instructions for the Commission. After she had altered and studied the proposal, it was presented for royal approval. The plan won the Queen's blessings and in May the work began.

Florence labored patiently with the Commission. She met daily with the group and either personally or by letter remained constantly in contact with the War Minister or other important members of the organization. She suggested witnesses and prepared briefs for examination and cross examination so that fair and complete evidence might be presented.

By August the Commission finished its work, and in January of 1858 the findings were made public. The group sustained Florence's contentions and showed that the mortality of the army in England was the result of neglect and inefficiency. It pointed out, for instance, that in one London district the civilian death rate was 2.2, whereas in the barracks, located in the same section, the rate soared to 10.4, and in another sector of England the rate among the soldiers hovered at 17.5, whereas the civilian rate lingered near the 3.3 mark.

The prevalent belief was that if the findings were publicized before action had been taken to rectify the appalling conditions the general reaction would be unfavorable. Hence publication of the report was delayed for months, during which time the reformative regime was initiated. Consequently four subcommissions were established to organize the barracks, to introduce a statistical department, to establish a medical school, to reconstruct the Army Medical Department so as to revise hospital regulations and to draw up a warrant for the promotion of medical officers.

These proposals were sent to the Bison, Lord Panmure, on August 7, but months passed before he was able to rouse himself from his customary inertia and begin the task. By January, 1858, Florence was preparing to stage a public tantrum if action was not taken. She wrote to Sir John McNeill:

"We have seen terrible things in the past three years, but nothing to my mind so terrible as Panmure's unmanly and stupid indifference on this occasion. I have been three years serving the War Department. When I began there was incapacity but not indifference. Now there is incapacity and indifference. That India will have to be occupied by the British I suppose there is no question. And so far from the all-absorbing interest of this Indian subject diminishing the necessity of immediately carrying out the reforms suggested by our Commission, I am sure you will agree that they are now the more vitally important to the very existence of the army."

Under the pressure of anxiety and mental strain Florence's health became increasingly poor and she was on the verge of a complete breakdown. Her physician sent her to Malvern for rest and seclusion, but this did not stop her work. She wrote, "The man here put me, as soon as I arrived, on a sofa and told me not to move and to take no solid food at all until my pulse came down. I reminded myself of a little dog, a friend of mine, who barked himself out of an apoplectic fit when the dog-doctor did something he had always manifested an objection to. Now I have written myself into a palpitation."

So serious was Florence's condition that her sister wrote, "She does not sleep two hours in the night, and continues most feverish and feeble." The valiant nurse who had been divinely appointed to her task refused to consider her physical weakness and gave attention to it only so far as it hampered her achievement of army medical reform.

"She goes down for half an hour into a parlor," continued Parthe, "to do business with a commissioner. It throws her back more to put off work for the 'cause' she lives for than to do a little every day . . . She is killing herself with work . . . It is an intolerable life she is leading, lying down between whiles to enable her just to go on, not seeing her nearest and dearest because, with her breath so hurried, all talking must be spared except what is necessary, and all excitement, that she may devote every energy to the work."

This is the spirit of which martyrs are made, and Florence was willing to lay down her life that the blunders of the Crimea might not be repeated. Writing to the War Minister near the end of 1857, she gave instructions as to how the fight should be conducted "when I am dead": "I hope you will have no chivalrous ideas about what is 'due' to my memory. The only thing that can be due me is what is good for the troops. I always thought thus while I was alive and am not likely to think otherwise now that I am dead." She referred, of course, to the fact that these instructions were to be carried out only in the event she died.

Her heart had been given to the Crimea, where there were the graves of many boys whom she had sought desperately to nurse back to health. She told her sister of her last wish: "The associations with our men amount to me to what I never should expect to feel—a superstition which makes me wish to be buried in the Crimea, absurd as I know it to be. For they are not there."

A lonely grave in the Crimea was not God's plan for
Florence, however. He willed that she complete the noble
work of alleviating human suffering, training nurses and
showing an example of spiritual valor to other nations.

On May 11, 1858, the House of Commons discussed
Florence's campaign for reform and her plans won un-
animous approval. Said Sir John McNeill concerning this
victory, "You have not labored in vain . . . You have made
your talent ten talents, and that to you, more than to any
other man or woman alive, will henceforth be due the welfare and efficiency of the British army."

Spurred on by this achievement, she threw her energies
anew into the battle. "Our soldiers enlist to death in the
barracks," the valiant reformer declared as she went forth to
crusade for the health of the army at home and on the
battlefield.

When the Commission's findings were made public, Florence supported and publicized them wholeheartedly through
the press and personal approval. But of course between the
fulfillment and the birth of these plans there was a slow
and tedious process of experimentation. Eventually Florence
won the battle against military leadership and as a result of
her efforts, provisions were made for reform. The warfare
had been long and hard but Florence experienced the joy of
seeing numerous changes.

The barracks were ventilated and heated, drainage was
introduced or improved, the water supply was extended,
kitchens were remodeled, gas lights were used instead of
candles and condemned buildings were reconstructed. At
Aldershot a school of practical cookery was established to
train hospital cooks in the preparation of wholesome and
energy-building meals for the wounded.

One of the subcommissions most tangled in red tape was
the group whose purported duty was to establish an army
medical school. Florence's ire was aroused.

"Formerly young men were sent to attend the sick," she

said in desperation, "and wounded soldiers who perhaps had never dressed a serious wound or never attended a bedside, except in the midst of a crowd of students, following in the wake of some eminent lecturer who certainly had never been instructed in the most ordinary sanitary knowledge, although one of their most important functions was hereafter to be the prevention of disease in climates and under conditions whose prevention is everything and medical treatment little or nothing."

Gradually other reforms followed. The principle, novel at that time, that the Army Medical department should care for the soldier's health as well as for his sickness, became the foundation of this work. A code defining the duties of commanding and medical officers in relation to the soldier's health was prepared as a result of this policy.

To safeguard the soldiers' moral health, reading and recreational rooms, coffee shops and lecture halls were furnished. Outdoor and indoor recreation facilities were also provided.

The battle, long and trying, had been won and Florence had achieved a moral victory. But there were new fields to explore. The vision beckoned and Florence followed the gleam.

Chapter 9

THE MOTHER OF MODERN NURSING

NEVER HAD THE CARE of the sick and wounded been an exact science, but Florence Nightingale resolved to establish nursing as a profession worthy of respect.

Florence Nightingale achieved her desire to become the mother of modern nursing. The greatness of her character, her keen mentality, her nobility of spirit—these she poured into the task.

During this period, though her health was waning rapidly, she found occasion to inspect, at Lord Panmure's suggestion, the plans for the first general military hospital to be constructed at Netley. The basic blueprints were virtually completed when the plans were submitted to Florence, but at once she saw that they were the work of men unacquainted with the problems of nursing the sick and wounded, and she bravely demanded that they be altered to conform to the needs she had experienced in the Crimea.

Florence gathered facts to sustain her position and consulted specialists, but Lord Panmure went his stubborn way. This led Florence to believe that the difficulty was caused not only by the lazy Lord Panmure but also by a lack of public information. Accordingly she laid plans for a public-enlightenment campaign which would present the problem of nursing to the humblest home in the nation. In October, 1858, at the Social Science Congress she contributed two papers on the subject of hospital construction. From that time her ideas became concrete in modern hospital construction.

During this period she felt the urge to foster more diligently the establishment of a nurses' training school. More than a quarter of a million dollars had already been subscribed and Florence directed Sidney Herbert, chairman of the fund, to invest this to the best advantage, for at the time her health would not permit her to undertake the heavy work involved.

During this time of recuperation her active mind was occupied with the preparation of a practical manual on nursing which should become a home encyclopedia as well as a doctors' and nurses' handbook on the subject. By the end of 1859 she had finished her *Notes on Nursing,* which became an international "best seller" that broke language barriers on the Continent and demanded a place on the reading list of the American public.

Having completed this valuable service, Florence devoted her attention to the founding of a training institute, which she decided should be conducted in connection with an established institution. Already active and functioning efficiently was St. Thomas' Hospital in London, to which Florence allotted two-thirds of the Nightingale Nursing Fund. The remainder of the money was given to King's College Hospital for the maintenance and training of midwifery nurses, for which there was an urgent demand in rural England. Accompanying the contribution to St. Thomas' Hospital was the stipulation that the nurses trained there should agree to serve in public hospitals and infirmaries.

In May, 1860, advertisements were published in leading papers and on June 24, fifteen probationers selected from the applicants were admitted.

This June day became the birthday of modern nursing, of which Florence Nightingale was the mother. Though pressed by many duties, Florence devoted much energy to the work, for she was answering a divine call.

On an upper floor of a new wing accommodations were provided for the probationers. Each had a bedroom and the girls shared a sitting room. During the first year each probationer was given room and board plus fifty dollars and the girls agreed to be subject to the rules of the hospital and to serve as assistant nurses in the wards. Their training was to be directed by doctors and graduate or regular nurses, a practice which prevails today.

Florence found an able assistant in Mrs. Wardroper, matron of the hospital, who for twenty-seven years had served as superintendent of the Nightingale School. "Her power of organization or administration," said Florence in describing the friend, "her courage and discrimination in character, were alike remarkable. She was straightforward, true, upright. She decided. Her judgment of character came by intuition, at a flash . . . yet she rarely made a mistake."

The first class graduated in 1861, and as the movement grew, other hospitals called for and received the graduates to serve on their staffs and as superintendents. The profession of nursing rose rapidly in public esteem. In the British colonies, the United States, Germany, France, Austria and other countries the "Nightingale idea" clamored for attention. At the outbreak of the Civil War the mere mention of her name evoked words of admiration. American women observed her example and studied her plans to guide the nursing of their sick and wounded.

Our nation organized a sanitary commission for which Florence Nightingale had provided the pattern. Her name became a household word, and the American soldiers revered her. Many were the eulogies honoring her and the Nightingale Training School.

In addition to giving the world trained nurses and providing a pattern for other nations to follow in establishing nurses' training centers in connection with their hospitals,

Florence raised nursing to a professional status and opened a challenging sphere of service for women. In England this was a more difficult task than in America, for in Britain, centuries of custom had shackled popular opinion. In our country, however, the Nightingale plan was received eagerly.

Despite her many duties, Florence had time to weep over the loss of her gracious friend and ally, Sir Sidney Herbert, who died on August 2, 1861. As Minister of War he had labored indefatigably to introduce and accomplish her reforms. Unmarried, she relied upon the strength of the many noble men who helped her achieve her goal.

"So few people know in the least," she wrote her father, "what I have lost in him. He takes my life with him. My work, the object of my life, the means to do it, all in one, depart with him."

When critics attacked Herbert's work in the War Office, Gladstone appealed to Florence for help in fighting it. At once she wrote *A Memorandum on Sidney Herbert's Work as an Army Reformer*. Having completed this, she left the Burlington Hotel, where she had set up her "Little War Office," and went to live in Hampstead, where she hoped to form new friendships and try to forget her departed friend.

Florence was, however, unable to escape remembering him, and on November 2 she wrote to her family concerning her grief: "My dear friend has been dead three months today. Poor Lady Herbert goes abroad this week . . . and shuts up Wilton. It is as if the earth had opened and swallowed up even the name which filled my whole life."

Work eased her sorrow. Perturbed by the alarmingly high death rate among the soldiers of the British army in India, Florence wrote a report which hinted at a reformation in the Indian campaign.

"On the mere question of climate," she wrote, "it is surely within human possibility, even in the majority of instances, so to arrange the stations and so to connect them, by railroads and telegraphs, that the troops would hardly be required to occupy unhealthy districts . . . The observance of sanitary laws should be as much a part of the future regime of India as the holding of military positions or as civil government itself."

When Florence could take time from her hospital work, she began a campaign, despite obstacles and government resistance, for reformation in the Indian army. A Royal Commission was established to study the problem, and Florence collected evidence and data regarding the Indian Army. This supporting evidence was authentic. When the Commission received its replies from India it often sent vanloads of mail to Florence for analysis.

When the report appeared, much of which was her work, it consisted of a two-thousand-page volume, printed in small type. This gave Florence the status of an ex-officio army general and brought a stream of officers, secretaries and ministers from the War Office to her for counsel. Having solved the problems of the army in India, Florence turned her attention to improving conditions and providing nursing care for the sick among the poor.

"I am sure you will be glad to hear," she wrote on September 26, 1864, to Sir John Lawrence, Viceroy of India, who was deeply interested in information concerning the homeland, "that one of my lifelong wishes, viz., the nursing of workhouse infirmaries by proper nurses, is about to be fulfilled . . . We undertake next month the Liverpool Workhouse Infirmary (of a thousand beds)—the first workhouse that has ever been nursed—with fifteen head nurses, trained by ourselves, and a lady matron who underwent a most serious course of training at our Nurses' School at St. Thomas' Hospital, fifteen assistants and fifty-two ex-pauper women whom we are to train as nurses. I am sure it is not for us to talk of civilization.

"For I have seen in our English workhouse infirmaries, neglect, cruelty and malnutrition such as can scarcely be surpassed in the semibarbarous countries. And it was then I felt I must found a School of Nurses for Workhouses."

Conditions in these infirmaries were as unsanitary and inhumane as those she had encountered in the army. She observed overcrowded sick wards, lack of sanitation and indescribable filth. Basins, towels, brushes and combs were lacking, and the dirty dishes were covered with maggots. Paupers served as nurses, and many of them stole the stimulants prescribed for the patients. Often the beds were unmade for seven days, and it was not uncommon for the patients to go without food for an entire day.

Florence, determined to correct these appalling conditions, demanded action, investigated mismanagement, pulicized her findings and drafted comprehensive plans for improvement.

The bill for reforming nursing in the workhouses was passed on March 29, 1867. This action provided that all unions and parishes be formed into one district for the treatment of the insane and fever and smallpox cases, which hitherto had been banished to the workhouse infirmaries. Separate infirmaries were formed for the noninfectious sick, dispensaries were established, a poor fund was established for the maintenance of asylums, the supplying of medicine and the care of pauper children in separate schools. So important was Florence's work in the achievement of these aims that both houses of Parliament praised her.

Still, in the midst of all this, as she viewed the huge unfinished task, she felt as if she were attempting to extinguish a raging fire with a medicine dropper. "Never think," she recorded in her notes, "you have done anything effectual in nursing in London till you nurse not only the sick in workhouses but those at home."

Already she was energetically considering this new and more vexing challenge, a task she had undertaken in her childhood days at Lea Hurst and Embley when, with a basket on her arm, she went sick-visiting.

"Nursing, especially that most important of all its

branches," she wrote regarding this vital issue, "nursing
of the sick poor at home, is no amateur work. To do it as it
ought to be done requires knowledge, practice, self-abnega-
tion and direct obedience to and under the highest of all
Masters and from the highest of all motives . . .

"It is an essential art of the daily service of the Christian
Church. It is destined by God's blessing to supply an opening, the great value of which in our densely-peopled towns
has been unaccountably overlooked until within these few
years."

This activity culminated in 1868 in the founding of the
East London Nursing Society, which promoted the movement
with such power that six years later the National Nursing
Association was formed, the purpose of which was to provide trained nurses to care for the poor who were sick in
their homes and to establish a district nurses' training
school in conjunction with a London hospital.

"As to your success," Florence wrote to the honorary
secretary of the Association, Florence Lees, "what is not
your success? To raise the homes of your patients so that
they never fall back again to dirt and disorder—such is
your nurses' influence; to pull through life-and-death cases,
cases which it would be an honor to pull through with all the
appurtenances of hospitals or of the richest in the land, and
this without any sickroom appurtenances at all; to keep
whole families out of pauperism by preventing the home
from being broken up and nursing the breadwinner back
to health."

Florence believed that under God she had been divinely
commissioned to give the benefits of nursing to the entire
population. She became a crusader, energized by the Holy
Spirit's power, which she sought daily through prayer, and
she labored in the confidence that she was divinely called
to a task as important as that of a missionary or other worker
in God's kingdom. In childhood she had received her call
from the Almighty, and now, in middle age, she was resting

calmly upon God's promises that He would never leave her nor forsake her as in the Master's Name she gave a cup of cold water to a poor sufferer.

In 1876 through the London *Times* she made a heroic plea for the establishment of a home for nurses in connection with the National Society for Providing Trained Nurses for the Poor. Courageously she championed the cause of the nurses, many of whom were underpaid and poorly housed.

"If you give nurses a bad home," she said, "or no home at all, you will have only nurses who live in bad homes, or no home at all. The district nurse should know how to nurse the home as well as the patient and for that reason should live in a place of comfort herself, free from the discomforts of private lodgings."

The Central Home for Nurses was established as a result of Florence's concern for them. The project progressed so favorably that in Queen Victoria's Jubilee Year, the larger portion of the sum presented as the Woman's Jubilee Gift, approximately a third of a million dollars, was devoted by the Queen to nursing the sick among the poor in their own homes. Branch centers for this work were established throughout the Empire, and Princess Christian became president of the association.

The many problems which occupied Florence Nightingale's attention multiplied, but no matter affecting public health escaped her notice. When the International Congress, which laid the groundwork for the Geneva Convention, convened, the government asked Florence to draft their instructions for action. This was a plan in which Florence was deeply interested and was a direct result of her Crimean work.

Societies under the Red Cross were soon organized throughout Europe and the remainder of the civilized world until the movement developed into volunteer nursing in wartime and later undertook philanthropic activities in national emergencies, catastrophes and disasters. Thus Florence

Nightingale was a guiding influence in framing the humanitarian principles upon which our Red Cross operates.

Nor was she too busy to give aid when the problem of the state regulation and control of vice and the elimination of vice centers demanded solution. Though the subject was odious to Florence, she gave the authorities the benefit of her observation and experiences in military life.

These heavy and energy-consuming tasks were accomplished by an invalid, for Florence was frequently bedfast. During these crowded days she suffered another loss, comparable to that of the death of Sidney Herbert, in the passing of poet Arthur Hugh Clough, long a trusted friend and helper. He had married Florence's cousin, but his devotion and assistance went beyond that of family ties. His ideals were high, and Florence found in his gentle disposition, poetic outlook and sense of humor a sedative for her frequently perturbed spirit.

Clough's practical help proved invaluable, for he acted as a personal secretary and often made arrangements for her long journeys. Occasionally he served as Florence's escort. Florence entrusted him with the responsibility of printing her numerous reports and articles, and conscientiously he read proofs. No matter what the task to be performed, she could always depend upon him to accomplish it. Thus he saved her many weary hours of labor and was always at hand when emergencies arose.

"I have always felt," she wrote after his death, "that I have been a great drag on Arthur's health and spirits, a much greater one than I should have chosen to be if I had not promised him to die sooner."

For months so great was the burden laid upon her tender spirit by Clough's passing that she was not able to open a newspaper lest she see his beloved name. Several years later when the poet's wife sent her a book, Florence wrote, "It would be impossible for me to read it or look at it, not from want of time or strength, but from too much of both spent on his memory, from thinking not too little but too much of him. I cannot bear to see a portrait of those who are gone."

During these years her heart was moved with compassion and love for her friends, and she could not conceal her feelings. She wrote to Madame Mohl in Paris, "I would mount three widow's caps on my head for a sign, and I would cry, 'This is for Sidney Herbert,' 'This is for Arthur Clough' and 'This, the biggest widow's cap of all, is for the loss of all sympathy on the part of my dearest and nearest.' "

Florence Nightingale lived a radiant life which glowed with love for her work, affection for those who bore her burdens, compassion for the sick and wounded and above all a passion to serve her God, with whom she communed as an ever-present Friend who gave her counsel and advice.

Florence realized that though her loss of these noble friends was great, theirs was a happier lot in the land where "they shall hunger no more, neither thirst any more . . . and God shall wipe away all tears from their eyes . . ." She said of Clough's death, "I am glad to end a day that can never come back, gladder to end a night, gladdest of all to end a month . . . I never see the spring without thinking of my Clough. He used to tell me how the leaves were coming out . . . Thank God, my lost two are in a brighter spring than ours."

She had been a companion of the nation's best and highest and had been sustained in her strenuous daily tasks by the touch of the Master's hand on hers. When the time came for her to shift from her shoulders the care of the wounded and the sick, she was ready to enter the Master's presence and hear His "Well done, thou good and faithful servant . . ."

Chapter 10

"EVEN DOWN TO OLD AGE . . ."

FLORENCE'S YEARS of acheivement were fast drawing to a close. She had worked with such energy during the Crimean War and the following years of reform in England that she was unable to participate in the fast-moving drama which took place during the next forty years. During these four decades she was an invalid who spent the days in almost complete seclusion.

During this time the world came to her door but was refused entrance. She could not forget the terrible siege of the Crimea, and the furrows of Scutari's memories were deep.

To the end of her life, Florence drank deeply of the joys and pleasures of service. She had but one motto, ". . . work, work, work," and work she did, inspired by the conviction that her calling was divine.

Florence was guided constantly by faith in the supernatural. She concluded a story entitled *Cassandra*, believed to be autobiographical, with this characteristic statement: "I believe in God." An independent thinker, she cut her way through the intricacies of form and custom and the red tape of regulations, yet she never lost her sense of dependence upon God.

Although she was a member of the Church of England, no creed or denomination could confine her within its bounds, for she felt a oneness of spirit with all churches and groups who did the will of the Heavenly Father. "All our actions, all our words, all our thoughts," she wrote, in speaking of the source of her religious faith, the spring of her energies, "the food upon which they are to live and have their being is to be the indwelling presence of God, the union with that God . . ."

Throughout her writings one detects her longing for spiritual uprightness, but equally evident is her realization that she came far short of the ideal. "It is what I have seen of the misery and worthlessness of human life . . . together with the extraordinary power which God has put into the hands of quite ordinary people, if they use it, for raising mankind out of this misery and worthlessness, which has given me this intense and ever-present feeling of the eternal life leading to perfection for each and for every one of us through God's laws."

She castigated herself heavily for impatience, selfishness and lack of confidence in God's guidance. Her meditations and writings on religion reveal her remorse and repentance as she considered her shortcomings. Writing to a friend, she said, "What a reprobate I am! A soul which has really given itself to God does His will in the present and trusts to the Father for the future. Now it is twenty years today since I entered public life and I have not learned that lesson yet."

Again she said, "Wretch that I was not to see that God was taking from me all human help in order to compel me to lean on Him alone. O Lord, even now I am trying to snatch the management of Thy world out of Thy hands . . . Too little have I looked for something better and higher than Thy work, the work of Supreme Wisdom . . . O God, to Thy glory, not to mine, whatever happens, may be all my thought."

This sustaining faith in God must be translated into service for man. Her religious belief was the highest motive for her conduct. "They say to live with God," she affirmed in the midst of carrying the burdens of the nurses whom she was training, "is not merely to think of ideals, but to do and suffer for them." Nursing was to her a divine call, not merely a profession. Never did she relinquish her aim to give the world "an organization in which women can be trained to be housemaids of the Lord."

When she returned from the Crimea, had she taken a long rest and laid aside the active burdens of reform, perhaps she would have recovered her health, but during those years of intense and agonizing suffering in which she spent entire nights without sleep, and hour after hour walked the four miles of hospital beds, she had torn the foundation from her physical endurance. When she reached England she had become an invalid, but she refused to abandon her God-given task until the vision she had received had become concrete in reform.

While living in the Burlington Hotel, until Sidney Herbert's death, she was an invalid, and carried on her work through others. When she moved to Hampstead the precarious state of her health demanded that she go into extreme seclusion. From time to time she moved to various lodgings in London and suburbs, but in November of 1865, forty-five years before her death, her father's generosity provided a house on South Street where she remained until the end of her life. This was not far from the home of Parthe, who was now Lady Verney. During these years she visited Lea Hurst and Embley and stayed frequently in her sister's home. London, however, was her headquarters, for there she could be near the center of the nation's active life.

In April, 1861, when Florence was riding high on the waves of popularity, she received this communication authorized by Queen Victoria: "It has been arranged that an apartment at Kensington Palace shall be put into proper repair with a view to its being offered by the Queen to Miss Nightingale as a residence. I need not tell you how grateful it will be to the Queen's feelings, even in this slight degree, to be able to mark her respect for this most excellent lady, of whom everybody in this country must be proud."

The Queen's gracious offer, one which most people would have been proud to accept, was, however, respectfully declined by modest Miss Nightingale. She knew that although the social environment of the palace would be delightful, nevertheless it could never, like her home, become a workshop. Florence's work was her major interest.

"Drawing room! I have no drawing room," she wrote her father indignantly when he said he was sending furnishings for her drawing room. "It is the destruction of many women's lives."

While physically able to work, she did not fail to do so. She loved flowers, but only occasionally could her brother-in-law, Sir Harry Verney, persuade her to visit the near-by park or take her for a drive that she might see the famous rhododendrons. Only seldom did she permit herself this relaxation from her guiding policy, ". . . work, work, work." She was surrounded not by drawing room luxuries but by piles of books, stacks of letters, masses of pamphlets, heaps of notes.

Her workbench eventually became a couch. Occasionally she received the most important visitors personally and dressed for the occasion, but the effort left her exhausted. Whenever possible, visitors were received in another room and Florence communicated with them by means of notes. She visited with her father more frequently than with any other member of the family. Those who were permitted personal visits often found her stronger than they had expected.

"Chadwick and Sutherland to dinner," said her father after a visit, "the former protesting that Flo's voice alone is sufficient to show that her (so-called) heart complaint is doubtful. In truth, she still seems to work like a Hercules, in spite of her weakness."

These visits left her trembling and weak, even before the death of her father in 1874, and eventually she became more strict regarding those admitted to see her. Letters from friends sometimes alluded humorously to this. Lady Ashbuton, a close and old-time friend, wrote, "I wish that you would let me sit like a rat in the corner while you are at dinner. It is much wholesomer not to eat in solitude. But I know I shan't get in, so I can only leave this at the door." The daughter added a note, saying, "Mother bids me add a P.S. and ask with her dear love if you could see her any time today. She will talk through the keyhole and not detain you five minutes."

Florence often entertained friends in her South Street home, though she saw little if any of them. Under her supervision and guidance, maids and servants provided for the visitors' comfort and pleasure. If a caller required a special diet, Florence planned the menu herself, and even wrote the recipe for an appealing dish. Frequently she sent for her sister or a close friend to entertain a guest so that there might not be a dull moment or that the visitor's special wish might be granted.

Many noted callers came to her home. Garibaldi, the famous Italian, of whom she was an admirer, was among them. Though it was an effort she entertained him personally. Writing to Harriet Martineau concerning the meeting, she said, "We had a long interview by ourselves. I was struck with the greatness of his noble heart . . . and with the smallness of his administrative capacity"—a field in which Florence excelled. "He reminds me of Plato. He talks about the ideal of good and the ideal of bad, about his not caring for republics or for monarchies. He wants only the right. Alas! Alas! What a pity—that utter impracticality."

Frequently Florence had royal visitors, but even for them she did not relax her rule of seclusion unless they had a personal and practical interest in hospitals and nursing. Otherwise she was not "well enough to receive them" unless they came unattended and without ceremony. Among her royal callers were the then Queen of Prussia, the Queen of Holland, Princess Alice and Crown Princess Victoria. With these she carried on interesting and helpful conversations regarding hospitals and related subjects.

The stream of her correspondence was constant. Friends and relatives took this burden from her shoulders, particularly her Uncle Sam Smith, who had accompanied her as far as Marseilles on the famous trip to the Crimea. Serving as Florence's secretary, he enjoyed her scribbled notes and comments on the margins of letters, which served as instructions for his replies. In reply to a woman who "loved and honored and hoped to see her someday," Florence directed, "Dear Uncle Sam, please choke off this woman and tell her I shall *never* be well enough to see her, either here or hereafter."

At various times Uncle Sam chuckled over such instructions as these :"I will give 21s. provided they don't send me any more of their stupid books, and don't let this unbusinesslike woman write any more of these unbusinesslike letters." "Choke her off. My private belief is she only wants a chance of getting married."

Speaking of a rambling and vague letter, she said, "The curious thing is that she does not seem to know whether it is a parent or a child that is lost." To a person who wrote concerning a secret cure, Florence commented, "What would they think of me did I possess such a discovery and kept it secret?"

On the second floor of her South Street home, in a living room and bedroom at the rear of the house, during these years Florence accomplished her daily work and the interviews she deemed wise to conduct. The apartment was pleasant. The bedroom had a curved outer wall and French windows. Shelves of books were conveniently placed, and flowers, of which she was exceedingly fond, brightened the little apartment. The walls were white and the rooms, curtainless, were flooded with light and blossoms.

The visitor was fascinated by the daintiness, the charm and the grace of the room. When not in bed, Florence sat in a large armchair. The drawing room, furnished in a more severe style, was given dignity by fine engravings and photographs of the Sistine ceiling, which Florence had admired since her girlhood visits to the famous chapel.

She was usually dressed in soft black silk. A shawl was thrown over her feet, and she wore a transparent white kerchief which was tied under her chin.

Though unable to engage in active work, she was not mentally indolent, and wrote profusely. This frail woman produced nearly a hundred and fifty published works. Some of these publications were privately circulated among friends, and many were printed at her own expense. Had she desired to turn her attention to writing, all evidence indicates that her excellent literary style would have enabled her to achieve success.

In 1874, Parthe visited her father, and when she wished him "Good night," the eighty-year-old man said, "Say not 'Good night' but in some brighter clime 'Good morning'." Two days later Florence was shocked by the news of his death, a loss which gave her great grief. He was the first member of the family to encourage her aspiration to become a nurse, and he was the one person whom she never excluded from her rooms. She wrote him often, saying, "I shall always be well enough to see you. As long as this mortal coil is one and at all . . . I shall keep all Sunday vacant for you. I should like to see you twice."

The hours spent with his gracious and famous daughter were among William Nightingale's most vivid and pleasant recollections.

Six years later, Florence, much weaker than when her father passed away, was again gravely shocked by the home-going of her ninety-three-year-old mother on February 2, 1880.

"February 2, 1880," Florence wrote a friend the following day, "my dear mother fell asleep just after midnight, after much weariness and painfulness. The last three hours were in beautiful peace, and all through she has been able to listen to and repeat her favorite hymns and prayers, and to smile as if she said, 'I am dying; it's all right.' Then she composed her ownself to death at nine last night, folded her hands, closed her eyes, laid herself down, and in three hours she was gone to a Greater Love than ours . . . Do you remember what Ezekiel said: 'And at even my wife died; and I did in the morning as I was commanded.' "

She prepared a card in memory of her parents' death on which she placed these words: "Live for Him; then come life, come death, we are His . . . God help us to use ourselves more entirely for Him in our work."

Day by day Florence lived the life of an invalid. She continued to receive a few visitors and penned on the margins of letters her cryptic remarks to guide those who managed her correspondence. In May, 1890, her sister, Lady Verney, died, and Florence was again burdened with sorrow.

"You have contributed," her husband wrote Florence, "more than anyone to what enjoyment of life was hers . . . Her love for you was intense. It was delightful to me to hear her speak of you and to see her face, perhaps distorted with pain, look happy when she thought of you."

There remained for her twenty years of life, although at times her mind was weak. Despite her invalidism, she reached the age of ninety. Though she did not use her poor health as an excuse for idleness, it saved her from foolishly squandering her time and wasting nervous energy.

Late in life Florence was to be blessed by two special honors. She was the first woman to receive from King Edward VII the Order of Merit. The King sent as his emissary Sir Douglas Dawson, who in December, 1905,

presented the honor at her home. The following year the
city of London gave her the Freedom of the City, a signal
honor reserved as a special tribute to the famous.

"The Lady with the Lamp" had brought the light of hope
and healing to battlefields, military camps, cottages and
palaces. Florence continued to carry the lamp, even though
the hand that held it was feeble. In the closing years of her
life, when visitors were permitted to see her, if they spoke
of nursing, her memory was dim, but when they spoke of
the soldiers, her face glowed with the joy of remembrance. It
was to these soldiers that she had given her heart.

On August 13, 1910, Florence slept peacefully away. The
Empire offered her burial in Westminster Abbey, but Florence's relatives, knowing her wish to be buried as a nurse,
refused this honor, and after a simple funeral service they
laid her away in the churchyard at East Wellow, beside
her father and mother. Her body was borne by six of her
"army children," which was as she would have wished it.

At the graveside her favorite hymn was sung—a hymn
which she never wearied of quoting to her nurses:

> The Son of God goes forth to war,
> A kingly crown to gain.
> His blood-red banner streams afar;
> Who follows in His train?

A four-sided monument marks the family grave, three sides
of which bear inscriptions concerning Florence's mother,
father and sister, and on the fourth is a small cross, the
letters F.N., and the words: *Born 1820. Died 1910.*

Throughout England and the world, memorial services
were held and monuments erected to honor this woman
who made nursing a dignified profession. Her picture is
found on hospital walls and she is honored wherever compassionate hearts and hands heal the wounded and suffering.

"Live your life while you have it," she counseled fellow
workers. "Life is a splendid gift. There is nothing small

in it, for the greatest things grow by God's law out of the smallest. But to live your life, you must discipline it. You must not fritter it away in fair purpose, erring act, inconstant will, but must make your thought, your work, your acts all work to the same end, and that end not in self but in God. This is what we call *character*."